Mortal Victory

By the same author:

THE LIFE OF S.T. COLERIDGE
SHINING MORNING FACE
BOY AND MAN

By Lawrence and Elisabeth Hanson:

THE FOUR BRONTËS
NECESSARY EVIL:
THE LIFE OF JANE WELSH CARLYLE
MARIAN EVANS AND GEORGE ELIOT
GORDON: THE STORY OF A HERO
THE NOBLE SAVAGE:
A LIFE OF PAUL GAUGUIN
THE PASSIONATE PILGRIM:
A VAN GOGH BIOGRAPHY
THE TRAGIC LIFE
OF TOULOUSE-LAUTREC
VERLAINE: PRINCE OF POETS

By Elisabeth Hanson:

MY POOR ARTHUR:
A BIOGRAPHY OF ARTHUR RIMBAUD

Mortal Victory

A Biography of
Paul Cézanne

Illustrated with photographs

by
Lawrence Hanson

HOLT, RINEHART AND WINSTON
NEW YORK

ND
553
C 33
H3

To

Number Fifteen

Contents

	Preface	ix
1	Beginnings	1
2	Toward Paris	18
3	Paris Interlude	33
4	End of a Banker	44
5	The Painter Appears	57
6	The Nonconformist	75
7	Hortense	94
8	Plein Air Painter	102
9	Impressionist	115
10	Laughingstock	123
11	Father and Son	138
12	The Outsider	146
13	Toward the Salon	154
14	Calm Before Storm	164
15	Infatuation	169
16	Death of a Man	174
17	Painter Succeeds Man	179
18	Mortal Victory	198
	Bibliography	233
	Index	237

Preface

Now, when Paul Cézanne has taken his place as one of the greatest painters of all time, is surely the moment for a revaluation of the man.

In the past much has been written about the painter, little about the man. If one is to believe this little, Cézanne was a misogynist who lived and died ungraciously. Standing before one Cézanne canvas after another, as I have done, this explanation appears inadequate; to me, such a man could not have painted the works now famed throughout the civilized world.

I therefore set out to try to discover Cézanne the man. What I found astonished me. I discovered with an amazement, which many readers of this book will share, that Cézanne resembled in his loneliness and in the tragedy of his life that painter who is everywhere loved and revered, Vincent van Gogh.

Yet not one of these admiring millions thinks twice about Paul Cézanne. Why? The answer is simple. Van Gogh wrote hundreds of long and fascinating letters. Those of Cézanne are few, short and, on the surface, unrevealing. Van Gogh died young and by his own hand. Cézanne lived into unromantic old age. Van Gogh left after his death a sister-in-law and nephew who dedicated their lives to make him and his work known to the world.

Cézanne left chiefly those who took pleasure in repeating adverse gossip.

No one troubled to clear away this gossip. No one commented on the difference between his work and the man ill will had created. That is why I have tried to portray Paul Cézanne and his life as they were in truth. The story is strange, infinitely sad, infinitely inspiring too. It can, I hope, be read for its own sake as a record of nobility in adversity. And although this book is not concerned with art criticism it may, I believe, lead readers to study and better appreciate Cézanne's work.

I have as always to thank all those generous helpers set down in previous books, a list of helpers headed by M. Roland de Margerie. And I have to express my appreciation of the work of two men. The biographies of Gerstle Mack are world famous; I, like everyone else who has read them, am indebted to them. Even more must I pay tribute to the work of John Rewald. No one can write on French painters of the second half of the last century without leaning heavily on his immense and scholarly labors.

For permission to reproduce illustrations I gratefully thank the Louvre, the Berner Kunstmuseum, Frau Ch. Bührle-Schalk, Mrs. Alexander Maitland, Dr. Grase and the Museum of Art in São Paulo, Dr. Hill, and the Courtald Institute, London.

—L.H.

CHAPTER ONE

Beginnings

1798–1858

IN the middle of the seventeenth century, a man carrying all his belongings on his back crossed the frontier of northern Italy and settled in the French town of Briançon. There he became known, as the habit then was, by the name of his birthplace, the small town of Cesana in Piedmont. As Italian pronunciation was difficult for the French, the name soon became corrupted; first it was Cesane, then Cezane, and finally the Cézanne which was to become world famous.

There was, however, nothing famous about the Cézanne who in the early 1700's moved down from Briançon to Aix-en-Provence. If he sought fortune there he did not find it; his son became a hairdresser in Aix and his grandson a tailor, both undistinguished. This last early gave up the fight and moved to the village of Saint-Zacharie, twenty miles from Aix. And there, on June 28, 1798, his son Louis-Auguste was born.

This son's future seemed likely to get no further than village tailoring. He, however, had other ideas. He grew into a powerfully built young man with brains and ambition. Unlike the rest of the villagers, he was not content to talk about their metropolis of Aix; he intended to get there and reestablish the family in their rightful center. Soon after the death of his father, in 1818, he acted. The manufacture of felt—one of the chief industries of Aix—had just begun to boom. The cause of this boom was the recent change in the fashions of men's and women's hats. Louis-Auguste quickly saw the possibilities of a flourishing business. Bringing with him the little money his parents had left him, he came to Aix and began to learn the trade. The difference between Louis-Auguste and most of the Aix businessmen was soon shown. After a year or two he came to the conclusion that he must get experience in Paris before setting up on his own. The decision made, he at once put it into practice. In those days Paris was almost as remote from Aix as Rome or Berlin, but he did not allow provincialism to deter him; he set off, obtained a job as hatmaker, then as salesman, with one of the leading manufacturers of felt hats.

After four years he had the business at his fingertips. He left for Aix with a fine record as hard worker and good salesman, and with two other men set up a hatshop in the Cours Mirabeau, the main street in Aix, and worked up a widespread export trade. This was in 1825. He was not made welcome—he was not Aix-born, he was a newcomer to the local trade, his years in Paris offended local pride, and his manner was blunt and countrified—but he had chosen his time well, he worked hard and proved himself shrewd. To the general envy his business grew fast. He made much money. After twenty years he had become one of the richest men of the town.

But by this time his ambitions had shifted. He had made his money rather more by the interest on loans than by the sale of hats. If he could profit to this extent by giving extended credit to the rabbit-producers who supplied him with felt, what could he not make if he controlled a bank!

His chance came three years later, in 1848, when the local bank failed. He bought it out for 100,000 francs—a very large sum at that time—and took into partnership the experienced cashier, a man named Cabassol. The bank prospered.

This startling success of the country-bred boy did not make life easier for him in Aix. Envy did not account wholly for this, nor did his birth outside the town, nor did his lack of the social graces. He had committed the sin which no provincial society could forgive. Some dozen years after coming to Aix he took as his mistress a sister of one of his employees, Anne-Élisabeth-Honorine Aubert. She was sixteen years younger than he and had once, it seems, worked in his factory. On January 19, 1839, their first child, Paul, was born in Rue de l'Opéra, a continuation of the Cours Mirabeau; two years later their second, Marie, in the Cours Mirabeau itself, in the house above the shop. Louis-Auguste had both children christened in his name, acknowledged them freely as his.

Two years after the birth of Marie he married their mother and set up house with her—the third and last child, Rose, was born in wedlock ten years after the marriage. But this gesture to respectability came too late. Aix society would have been unlikely to accept the low-born Anne (her people were all small tradesfolk) even had he married her at once; the delay of five years made certain of ostracism. The Cézanne home was a home where visitors were rare. Louis-Auguste, wealthy though he was, could not gain admittance to the public life of the town—in 1848 he was decisively, almost derisively defeated in an election for the municipal council. The Cézannes were and remained outsiders.

Louis-Auguste, a patient man, bided his time: he had been snubbed and rejected, but his son, backed by wealth and encouragement—what might he not do?

The story has been told many times of the way in which the banker dealt with defaulting clients. A debtor at Marseilles could neither pay interest nor repay the loan. Louis-Auguste settled down in the man's house, examined his accounts and, discovering him to be extravagant, regulated the daily budget, enforcing strict economy. Only when the household expenditure was reduced to a point which permitted the man to recommence paying interest on his loan did the banker return to Aix.

This story—not uncommon in those days of paternalism in business—has been held up as proof of Louis-Auguste's hardness and passion for money. What it more accurately shows is his reluctance to ruin anyone and his belief—well-founded even though often irritating—that he was a better organizer than most. He was essentially a product of the age of reason, and his home, though a sober one, was not unhappy. It was quiet because the man it was built around did most of the talking. Demonstrations of affection were rare because Louis-Auguste, though free with his tongue, had the peasant fear of any other kind of freedom. But it was held together by the pride with which the wife and children regarded him, a pride which ran easily into awe and a kind of fear. This self-made man of many words but cautious actions had his own dignity; his family responded to it. If he did not make many motions of love, all believed that he thought and acted for the good of all; a practical man, his affection would be practical too. If he, as the peg on whom all hung, exercised an unfortunate influence, it was because he was in some degree a disappointed man. He had done wonders, he could tell himself, but for him the making of money was not all. He wanted acceptance; he was accepted grudgingly. He wanted to take an active part in local politics—he was an advanced republican—and was snubbed. Driven back on himself until his son grew up, he took what consolation he could from his work and young family. The consolation was considerable; so too was the modicum of dissatisfaction left over. He became something of a recluse, difficult to approach. His own difficulty, to express emotion, got in the way of his happiness and in the way of the happiness of all who depended on him.

If the elder children, Paul and Marie, were happy at home, it was with a subdued happiness. They loved their mother but she was too obviously a cipher. Most of their admiration and respect went to their father, but admiration and respect are not the soundest base for an uninhibited childhood. They were pensive children notably lacking in self-confidence.

How far their illegitimacy affected them in the home is hard to say; they had no friends, but companioned each other. But life at school was a different matter. Paul's four or five small years in the Primary School in Rue des Épinaux were peaceful; the next three, in the École Saint-Joseph, were not. And when, as next step, he moved on as boarder to the Collège Bourbon he ran straight into trouble. In a town like Aix everything is known. Schoolboys fear and detest the unusual; even more than at the École Saint-Joseph, the boys at the Collège Bourbon, the voluble part of them, that is, were bullies of the worst type. Paul presented them with an ideal butt. Had he had charm he could have scotched the bullying quickly. But he had no charm; all he had inherited from his vivacious mother was her hot temper; he was stiff and awkward like his father but without the man's compensating self-assurance.

One thing saved him from a school life of absolute misery
—his physical strength, for he had followed his father in
this too; he was big and strong. He soon won peace, therefore; but it was a hurtful and harmful peace; to an emotional boy this negation of life was a kind of agony, driving him deeper into himself.

That he said anything at home of his sufferings is
unlikely; he had a fanatical pride, he was not one to un-
burden himself, and he had a terror of falling in his father's
esteem. So the elder Cézanne was not given the choice of
withdrawing his son or advising the boy to grit his teeth
and win his way through the ordeal. Grown suspicious,
Paul preferred to trust no one at school; he acted as he
believed his father would have acted, working grimly; he
would pass the baccalaureate, enter the bank and in due
course succeed his father.

In 1852, when Paul was thirteen, this life of endurance
suddenly and unexpectedly brightened. He met Émile
Zola. Émile was the son of a distinguished Venetian engineer and a French mother; born in Paris, he had spent
most of his childhood in Aix, where his father designed a
large dam, afterward known as the Barrage Zola, and
canal which were to supply the town with water. He died
suddenly in 1847, when Émile was seven and before the
dam could be completed, leaving his wife heavily in debt.
Madame Zola lost still more money in litigation, trying
to obtain payment for her husband's work, and by the time
Émile went to the Collège Bourbon she was living in poverty with her parents and could only afford to send him
as part boarder. This, however, was a blessing. He was
small, sharp, intelligent and with a mind of his own; the
school bullies fastened on him; he answered back, was
not interested in regulation games, in smut, in stupid
jokes; worst of crimes, he had not been born in Aix. They

set themselves to make a misery of the life of this "Parisian." He was "sent to Coventry"; all the boys were forbidden to speak to him.

Then occurred one of those scenes often met with in school life. Paul, normally silent and apathetic, regarded the treatment of Émile Zola with an indignation that rose into a passion. He knew what it was to endure enforced silence, but he at least was big enough to look after himself, he (as he told himself in his modesty) had little to offer. Émile was not only defenseless but charming and obviously gifted. In a fit of rage, Paul defied the ban and spoke to Émile. He was set on and thrashed. Obstinate, he again spoke to the outcast. This time he got his way. The bullies tired of their sport and left the two boys alone.

This apparently uncharacteristic action was decisive. The grateful Émile took the friendless boy under his wing, intellectually speaking, and offered him an affection so open and without reservations of any kind that even the suspicious Paul surrendered. Émile showed not only gratitude but perception; the dour, difficult Paul, shooting doubtful glances from under his eyes, was not at first or even second sight a promising subject for attention; but Émile, lonely and unpopular himself, somehow penetrated the unattractive guard and sensed a passionate heart. More extraordinary, he sensed the artist in this sullen plodder. Charming, expressive, and ambitious, he set himself to open the eyes and the heart of this new friend.

He succeeded to an astonishing degree. He and Paul not only became fast friends, spending every possible minute of the day together, but formed the nucleus of a school intelligentsia, a tiny set but lively. Precocious in some ways they were, priggish they were not. At their head was the small Émile, the brain and begetter of enthusiasms, and by his side the large, shambling Paul, two inseparables. A third, Baptistin Baille, one year younger than Émile, two years younger than Paul, attached himself with southern fire. For the next six years the boys, two always, three usually, lived out of school hours a life of joyous adventure cast in a well-nigh perfect setting.

2 ⤳

The thousands of travelers who take the great national routes 6 and 7 from Paris to the south every year pass through Aix toward the end of their journey. They pass with reluctance. Aix is the heart of Provence and if shorn of its old glories when Provence was a kingdom and the literary center of Europe, it has gained new ones—spacious avenues of historic houses built in the warm stone of the neighboring mountain, fountains at every hand, vivid speech and gesture, richly varied shops under bright awnings, all and more wrapped in the heat and color of the south. There the traveler realizes for the first time and with a thrill of delight that he has reached the Mediterranean country.

Yet the man who passes through the town on his way to the coast, or merely stops there overnight, misses one of its greatest treasures. He comes to Aix and leaves it over an all but featureless plain. To the north, guarding the town from cold winds, stands the long expanse of Mont Sainte-Victoire. This apparently bleak stretch of hill rising abruptly out of the plain is within sight of the traveler and his only notable horizon for many miles; but of the country between Aix and the mountain he sees and can imagine nothing. It was here, in these few magical miles, that Paul, Émile and Baille spent the happiest years of their lives; years which in one case settled the destiny of the boy and gave the world a great painter.

Nothing, however, was further from the mind of Paul Cézanne than painting as day after day of vacation, evening after long evening of spring and autumn, morning after early morning of every season in the year he rambled through this wooded country leading to the Sainte-Victoire. The excursions usually began before daybreak. At three o'clock the first to awaken and dress himself would hurry round to the homes of his friends and hurl stones at the shuttered bedroom window until the sleeper awoke, threw himself into some clothes, seized the haversack ready packed with food and books by his bedside, and joined him.

Eagerly walking, often running until beyond the ancient ramparts, the boys explored the deep wooded ravines into which few people ever ventured, pushing a way through the brambles with the triumphant air of men subduing virgin territory. In the height of summer the morning would end on the bank of the river Arc where, stripping, they plunged into the cold and rapid water with shouts, songs, splashings that drove the birds from the trees in a flurry of wings. Then to lunch, which they cooked and ate on the spot, one lighting a fire of twigs, another spitting the meat, a third preparing the salad. When provisions were low they would supplement the meal from the river, casting lines or, if their hunger could not endure even that delay, catching the fish with the bare hand held stealthily under water in a shallow rocky pool. Lunch done, they lay prone under a tree to escape the beating sun, reciting poetry or acting out a play. At first the classics held them and the sonorous verses of Homer or Virgil would sound out enthusiastically into the still air. Then they discovered Victor Hugo and, surrendering instantly to the pompous rhetoric, repeated with a fervor poems learned by heart, or declaimed, strutting and throwing attitudes, the bombast of *Ruy Blas* or *Hernani*. As his adorers advanced into their middle teens, Hugo's reign was cut short by Musset, and romance of another kind reared its fair head; *Rolla* and *Les Nuits* were memorized and repeated time after time with a softer passion. The poems all were writing—for of course they would be poets—and which they recited to great applause, turned from gory battle scenes to the charms of some local damsel and to the state of their wildly beating hearts; hopeless love was the favored theme, and reader and audience looked as somber and wan as healthy, high-spirited boys were able.

On energetic days they pushed past ravine, river, and wood to the Sainte-Victoire itself. There, at its feet, was the dam designed by Émile's father, a tempting bathing place. There, too, were the yawning quarries cut out of the mountain and from which the town of Aix had been built. The quarries and the lower slopes of the mountain offered exciting scrambles which with hoots and yells the boys essayed. The dangers were not perhaps so extreme as imagination made them, but the friends slipped, shouted, and pushed higher with all the carefree gusto of the mountaineer born; they were the modern troubadours, at once muscled and melancholy, risking unloved lives for the honor and glory of their fair lady. That the lady was a leggy schoolgirl in Aix who persistently looked the other way mattered not at all; the hopeless suicidal desperation was everything. If the air in their nostrils intoxicated them, if the colors delighted their eyes, and the blood in their veins tingled with well-being, they were too often in their chosen role of the day to analyze the source of their happiness; that it came from a lifelong misery was satisfaction enough. Nor did they comment on the startling change of scene from river and ravine to the Sainte-Victoire. The country between Aix and the mountain was warm, rich, domestic in a wild way; the mountain stood with ribbed, gaunt side as though the very skeleton of the earth had been exposed; yet both appeared to the wanderers as playgrounds only, differing indeed, but the delight they afforded being all. Consciously, that is; for despite this youthful indifference to analysis, despite the soporific quality of the familiar, one of the band was unconsciously noting the difference and taking the Sainte-Victoire to his heart. Had he been told that this stern upthrust of rock was to change the face of painting he would have been amazed and incredulous. Had he been told that he was to be the agent of this change, he would have smiled ironically (he did not laugh easily) and gruffly change the subject.

In autumn the group of friends turned hunter; yet more because this falling in with the sportsmen of the town expressed manliness than any real desire. Paul and Émile were both tenderhearted and the formidable rifles slung across their back, the carefully dirtied game bags were mere camouflage; the guns did no more than fire an occasional pot-shot which the bird escaped not without scorn, and the game bags provided excellent cover for books of poetry, printed and manuscript. The outing was the thing, the companionship, the freedom, the exhilarating vows, the comfortable prophecies—for all were destined, they assured one another, for a great future in the arts.

On the rare frosty days of winter the little band, wild with excitement, tore along the hard, echoing roads to one of the outlying villages. There, with immense *sang-froid,* they would order an omelet at the local *auberge* before racing each other home. In bad weather they had a refuge in the attic of Baille's house in which they practiced amateur chemistry, wrote and acted their own plays, and scribbled and painted on a couple of battered easels. Paul and Émile both attended the school drawing and painting classes and Paul took lessons in drawing at the town academy, but of the two Émile was the more proficient and won the most prizes. It was in any event a game simply, an overflow of the immense vitality and lust for expression that filled them all. As was their music, for both Paul and Émile learned to play indifferently well, one on the clarinet, the other on the cornet, and tried their hands at any additional instrument they could get hold of. They even joined the town music club and played in the band, which turned out from time to time to greet the return of local celebrities from Paris. A more typical use of their instruments as they grew into their late teens was the serenading of a pretty girl—not, however, with much success.

Though their main pleaures were found out of school, all were surprisingly hard workers in it. Émile was good at everything, Baille very quick, Paul plodded along industriously and eventually took the lead in the classics, turning out Latin verses with quite an air; if not brilliant elsewhere he was sound in practically every subject. He gave the general impression in school of intending to make himself a worthy son of his father.

3 〜

The record of these years from 1852 to 1858 is, on the surface, one of hard work in school and of days and weeks and months of intense pleasure outside it. For two of the three friends this was an exact description of their lives; they enjoyed almost every minute of them. For the third, Paul, qualification is necessary. Bickerings and quarrels sprang up from time to time as with any group of schoolboys, but the shadow thrown by Paul on their outings

was of another kind, which puzzled and hurt. He worked
with a will and often played with a kind of gusto, but
not always. His hot temper, quickly assuaged, was acceptable in a country where sudden explosions of temperament were common. His black moods were quite another thing; without apparent reason his silence would
turn into a savage sullenness. There was no telling when
these depressions would fall on him, no telling when he
would break out and say bitter, wounding things. Émile
excused him by explaining that an evil demon had entered
his head which he was unable to control, and by remind-
ing Baille that he had a heart of gold and in understanding and aspiration was one of them to the hilt; and this,
though it explained nothing, eventually restored the
peace.

Émile, fond of Paul though he was, could never discover what caused these strange glowerings and sullen
outbursts; not surprisingly, since Paul himself had little
notion. His life had been full and rich since meeting
Émile, to an extent he could never have dreamed of. If
he lived under a kind of restraint at home, the restraint
of obligation and inexpressiveness, he was freed from
physical restraint to a remarkable degree, coming and
going almost as he pleased. Yet this compensation stopped
far short of bliss. Though Émile had worked wonders
with him, he could not perform a miracle; he had neither
changed Paul's nature nor had he been able to eradicate
the effect of the formative years.

Superficially Paul was merely personifying his country-
men. The people of the Midi, outwardly vivacious, are at
heart sombre and moody; when, a few years later, Vincent
van Gogh complained that the townsfolk of Arles were
all "a little cracked" because of the sunshine in which
they spent so much of their lives, he was saying no more

than the truth. But Paul was less fortunate than they; because their feelings are shallow they can disguise a natural moodiness; with Paul there could be no disguise; he wore his moodiness openly because it expressed a deeply passionate nature.

So even in the midst of years which any boy would envy he was haunted by obscure premonitions of failure and disaster. The stain on his birth, ground in by the early years at school, had soured a spirit not so much cowed as despairing in the face of a father at once admired and impossible to emulate. Yet he could not be the listless, conforming child so often found in the homes of strong-minded parents; he could not dismiss himself as a nonentity; meekness was a thousand miles removed from him. The struggle between this submerged but living will, passionate nature and absence of self-confidence could not be hidden indefinitely; it revealed itself in the moods found so inexplicable by his friends.

When he thought openly about it, Paul was inclined to blame his manner and appearance. He was absurdly sensitive. Though plain, he was not ugly. He had a round, rather pudgy face with the prominent and slightly hooked nose of his father. Over a low forehead thin black hair covered a well-shaped head; under it strong black eyebrows jutted over small eyes obliquely set. These eyes usually gave the impression of being half-closed, for he would often walk with head down or eyes veiled, fearing to draw attention to himself. His mouth was thin, bitter, obstinate, the lower lip curling down; a disturbing mouth, yet not so disturbing as the eyes at certain moments, the moments when the inner struggle emerged. Then the "demon" of Émile glared from the eyes of a fanatic as much as of a frustrated boy, black pupils burning out of a large white surround—eyes hard to meet, impossible to reason with.

Yet neither his looks, normally unobjectionable, nor his surly, evasive manner kept him solitary so much as the suspicion that he was peculiarly difficult and would cause trouble to any who associated with him. The more he longed for company the less chance he had of it, this being a law of life, until the happy day when, forgetting himself, he met the young Émile and had his reward in the leadership of that delightful young individualist.

The reward was great. During those six years he had hour after hour of unclouded happiness and, what was even more foreign to him, lightheartedness. Yet in some ways the association with Émile actually caused him moments of greater unhappiness than he had known during his isolation before meeting Émile. Surrounded by boys who showed unfriendliness or open contempt, he had at least the bitter comfort of believing them his inferiors. With Émile he could believe nothing of the kind. Yet even with Émile's encouragement he could not persuade himself that he was personable (in their vague encounters with local girls his excessive *amour propre* suffered one blow after another), and although he had rare moments of a kind of awkward loquacity, he was never able to express his emotions freely. He was known as Émile's "silent shadow," but the nickname fitted him in fact only; he was no toady or unthinking admirer but a person who could accept nothing without painful questioning. Inwardly, however; for his feelings were as imprecise as they were strong, as bedeviled by doubt as by lack of the gift of tongues. Émile unsettled him by vehement insistence on their extraordinary future—vehement but imprecise, since the young Zola had no idea how they

were to take the world by storm, only a certainty that they
would do so.

Paul did not need Émile to awaken a sense of being
destined for the unusual; he had had intimations of it
ever since he could remember; but his intimations turned
morbid under the optimistic reiterations of his so obviously gifted leader. For if Émile's cloudy assurances of
a glorious destiny inflated him in one breath, in the next
they depressed him to the earth; his friend, whom he
found almost perfect and whose self-confidence never
failed to astonish, merely emphasized the gulf between
them. Émile would go on to world triumph—nothing
could be more certain—while he . . . ! And at this
thought gloomy visions assailed him, the "demon" sparked
from those extraordinary eyes, and he flared into rage,
hatred, abuse.

Again, Émile declared a life of glory for them all.
And while it was anything but clear how the glory
was to be won, one inference could be drawn by any
intelligent boy; it was not going to be won on the field
of finance. What, then, was to become of the bank for
which Paul was educating himself so diligently, which
his father expected him to enter, and which he felt often
enough was the destiny to which he was called by inclination as well as duty? Yet there, day after day, was
Émile and his call to the arts; and he too, like Louis-
Auguste, awakened a loyalty that would not be betrayed.
Paul was not one to ask a question that he could not
answer. The question remained, however, bulking ever
larger as the hour of decision approached, blighting some
of the time he spent with his friends and more of the
time he spent alone.

So these six years, which spelled almost unalloyed
happiness and hope to Émile Zola and Baille, and which

for sheer joy in living have rarely been surpassed in the annals of boyhood, held for Paul a host of backward emotions. No wonder that he so often walked the streets with bent head and averted eyes; his premonitions were right in this, that he was not a favorite of fortune. Neither of the other two had serious misgivings about the general direction of their enthusiasms, neither was troubled by self-doubt, neither had a father to succeed who invited compliance through love, like-mindedness, and force of character which hung over the Cézanne household in the form of a wordless, expectant pride. That Paul alone should suffer at all in the midst of such halcyon years was sheer bad luck. Long before they had ended he was well on the way to greeting misfortune as a brother.

Nevertheless, even to him, mordant and mistrustful, these years appeared little short of absolute paradise, all imperfections erased at a blow, when in February, 1858, Émile told him suddenly that he had to go to Paris.

Toward Paris

1858–1861

WHEN the young Zola went off to finish his education at the expense of his mother's Parisian relatives, he left behind a Paul who was considered by his few friends as a budding poet; like the rest he had played at everything, but in poetry he showed a certain flair. Émile was soon bombarding him with letters of criticism and encouragement, demanding to be shown everything he wrote. He had decided to become a writer, but with less apparent reason than Paul, who had not decided to become anything.

Émile considered that his chief task was to keep Paul up to the mark and as soon as possible get him to Paris. This was partly selfishness; living with a mother still finding it difficult to make ends meet, he was having hard work to keep cheerful and had not found a friend to replace Paul; he preferred to suffer in company. It was partly vanity too, for Émile had a snatch of Napoleon in himself and enjoyed the molding of another life. But he was genuinely anxious to bring out the genius smoldering in his difficult friend.

Paul did not help him. Émile gone, he relapsed into moodiness. The leader away, the little group collapsed.

There were no more outings to the ravines or the Sainte-Victoire, no more readings or acting-out of plays. "Since you left Aix," Paul writes, "I have been weighed down by a deep melancholy." Aix itself he found "dull."

Émile refused to accept this inertia. What was Paul doing with himself? he wanted to know in almost every letter; and when he was sent poems he demanded that his friend should take more trouble with them. He was a better critic than poet and perceived that Paul's efforts were too obviously mere extensions of his letters, fluent at times, ironical almost always, serious never. He tried hard to make a great poet of him; tried tactfully, too; for even the masterful young Zola found it necessary to deal gently with the strange friend who depended so much on him. "You write for me," he says in one letter, "and I thank you for it. But the herd, my dear old chap, is more demanding. It is not enough to express, one must express well. . . . I ask myself what the good Cézanne lacks to make a great poet. Purity? He has good ideas, his form is strong and original, but the whole effect is marred by provincialism, solecisms etc."

That Cézanne had no heart for writing he did not guess. Cézanne was a genius in embryo, of that he felt sure; and how could he display this genius but in literature? The occasional drawings and water colors that filled up odd spaces in his friend's letters did not and could not provide a clue; even more than the poems, they were plainly nonserious. Cézanne himself could not help him since he continued to pass his days in a form of would-be ironical indecision, working hard for the baccalaureate he was due to take that summer as a stage leading to the bank.

In his guidance of Paul's romantic soul Émile was on safer ground; that is to say, he encountered no obstacle.

Like all young men morbidly conscious of physical and social failings, Cézanne dreamed of an angel of purity who would discern the passion behind the unlovely mask and mold him into her image. It was a romantic age and he and Zola had made a god of Michelet as well as of Musset; and in his search for a "pure, noble love" Paul had the moral support of his friend conveyed in many words. That was about the only satisfaction he did have. Zola, handsome and with an air, did not go unnoticed; his friend went empty, his life from this point of view consisting almost wholly of parading the streets discovering goddesses whom he never had the courage to address and who never so much as glanced at him. He did not ask much, merely the sight of an attractive girl. Sometimes he was content to dream about her and enjoy "a certain inner sadness." A certain pleasure, too, as when he wrote, "I dreamt that I held in my arms my lorette, my grisette, my darling, my little baggage, that I smacked her bottom and many other things besides. . . ." But these adolescent visions of himself daring one of the local prostitutes remained visions; he had neither the courage nor, when it came to the point, the desire to follow the lead of some of the elder college boys.

Occasionally, and less happily, his infatuations led him into the self-ridicule that came so easily. "I've had a passion for a certain Justine," he told Émile in a letter in which he aired his English. "She is truly 'very fine,' but as I haven't the honor to be 'of a great beautiful' she has always turned her head away from me. When I threw my peepers in her direction she used to lower her eyes and blush. Moreover, I remarked that when we found ourselves in the same street she used to turn round and slip away without looking behind her. *Quanto*

a della donna I'm not happy, yet I run the risk of meeting her three or four times a day. But there's something
richer to come, my dear chap: one fine day a young man
accosted me, a first-year student like myself, in brief the
Seymard you know. 'My dear fellow,' he said, taking my
hand, then attaching himself to my arm and continuing to
walk toward the Rue d'Italie. 'I'm going to show you'—
he went on—'a sweet little thing I love and who loves
me.' I declare that at once a cloud seemed to pass in
front of my eyes, that's to say I had a feeling that fortune
was not on my side, and sure enough as midday struck,
Justine emerged from her dressmaking establishment
and on my honor I had no sooner seen her than Seymard
with a gesture said, 'Here she comes.' "

He continues with further details of the familiar contretemps, then broke out with a plaintive, "Ah! what
dreams I have had! . . . I told myself, if she doesn't
dislike me we shall go to Paris the two of us, there I will
be an artist and we shall all be together. That way, I
said to myself, we shall be happy. I dreamed of the
pictures I should make, of my studio on the fourth floor,
of you with me. How we should enjoy ourselves! I
wouldn't ask for wealth, you know what I am, with a few
hundred francs I think we could live contentedly. . . ."

The occurrence, common to thousands of romantically-
minded and shy young men, is not so interesting as the
reference to painting. This reference, his first, was no
more serious than his infatuations; he was chiefly in
love with the idea of the life Mürger had just made
popular in his *Scènes de la Vie de Bohème;* it shows
that, as far as his dreams went, he had transferred his
role from that of starving poet to starving painter. And
that is all; for when he wrote this letter, in June, 1859,

all his practical thought was given to the rapidly approaching baccalaureate. And with some reason, for in the next month he failed to pass the examination.

He was saved from too much self-questioning by the arrival of Zola for the summer holidays. Stimulated immediately by his friend's brisk personality, he proposed to turn out a five-act play on Henry VIII of England; instead, he and Baille, temporarily reunited by the presence of the lively link, spent their days with Zola reviving the joys of their boyhood years. Carefree for the moment, Cézanne again swam, fished, walked, talked a little and listened a lot in the country he had come to love with a passion. The passion, like all his emotions, could not get itself expressed even in Zola's company. Yet even so early as this summer some instinct was comforting him with the thought that words, which came so inadequately and with such difficulty, were not necessarily the only or the best means of expressing this particular and overpowering love. There was another way.

There was no time to explore this way when Zola returned to Paris, even if Cézanne could have acquired the skill or summoned the resolution; another essay at the baccalaureate was hanging over him. In November he tried again and passed.

This success made him openly a momentary hero at home. It also led straight to unheroic behavior. His gratified father at once urged him to join the law school at the university; a degree in law would give the bank, and Cézanne family, a distinction that Louis-Auguste had failed to convey in person.

For the first time in his life Paul rebelled. He did not like the idea of the law school, was bored by the subject. But he did not refuse to go there; a plain negative to his father was more than he dared, more than he wished. So he joined the school, complained bitterly about it to Zola, and did as little work there as possible. This last he made simple; he joined the drawing academy, too, and spent most of his time there.

2 ～～～

This situation lasted for two and a half years. It deteriorated with every month that passed, yet even at the end there was no open break, since a break between Cézanne father and son was unthinkable to both. When Paul became liable for military service, on his twentieth birthday, his father at once bought him a substitute.

Zola continued his campaign by letter and pressed it still harder in person each time he came down for the summer holidays: Paul must come into the open, declare for the arts, throw to the winds his law studies and his future in the bank. To Paul, trying to please everyone and satisfying no one, this bold talk was a shade too facile, particularly from a young man who remained in his Paris school trying to pass the baccalaureate. He responded with a significant gesture; on one of their outings he made a painting of his friends dressed up as brigands. This was his first attempt at *plein air* painting, but Zola's pleasure in it was marred by the equally significant fact that Cézanne continued to complain of his law studies. Not until late in 1859, after Zola had twice failed his examinations, abandoned further attempts, and, deciding to devote his life to literature, worked at the docks to try to keep himself while he wrote—not until faced and shamed by this proof of sincerity did Cézanne seriously consider trying to join him.

In the Cézanne home all remained peaceful. To a point Louis-Auguste was an unusually broad-minded man for

his time, as his liaison and even more his marriage had
shown. With his son he took the view that as long as
he worked toward the desired end of banking, or, if he
preferred, a distinguished career in the law, he could do
just as he pleased with the rest of his time. Hence
Paul's years of freedom with Émile and Baille, and hence
the painting. When he joined the academy, his father was
tolerantly pleased for a man who did not know one painting from another; if Paul wished to learn to draw and
paint in his spare time he was welcome. And when Paul
began to bring home the copies he had made and his
mother fixed admiringly on the worst and hung it in her
room, when his sister Marie watched him at work and
praised him, his father was proud of this versatile son.
He even, in this year, helped to turn the boy into a
painter as well as to fix his affections in Aix, though he
did so unconsciously. For it was in 1859 that Louis-
Auguste bought one of the largest properties outside
Aix to use as a summer retreat during the hot months.
He paid 90,000 francs for it, a figure which gives a fair
idea of his wealth. The Jas de Bouffan was an estate of
nearly forty acres. The Arc ran through its thick woods,
in the center of which was one of the most beautiful
seventeenth-century houses for miles around, a house
backed by an avenue of venerable chestnut trees and
fronted by a tree-fringed lake. Paul, who had known the
estate for years, exploring it often with his friends, fishing
in the river, picnicking in the grounds, was overjoyed
when his father bought it. He painted there again and
again; the Jas de Bouffan is today, with the Sainte-
Victoire (which he could see, a perpetual hint of the
Cézanne "sensation," from the grounds of the house),
the most familiar subject of all Cézanne canvases.

Until the end of the year, then, harmony reigned in the

Cézanne home; if father and son were at cross purposes, the one did not know it, the other did not choose to see it. Then, pressed by a Zola who had taken the plunge, and emboldened by his growing hatred of the law, Paul spoke out. He wanted to be a painter. Louis-Auguste, amazed to discover that his son had been consistently avoiding the law school whenever possible for the last fifteen months, heard the reason with typical phlegm. They discussed the matter often and calmly. Louis-Auguste, like the peasant he was, advised caution: "Be careful, take your time, think before you act, never let emotion get control." This had been the motto of his life, and when he repeated "Before you go out be sure you know where you're going," and similar saws, he genuinely believed that the emotional Paul needed the advice. How, he asked, after a bare year at the academy, could he be sure that painting rather than banking was his life's work? And when Paul, repeating the kind of phrase so often employed during the summers with Zola, began to talk about the call of genius, his father not turning a hair, replied that genius, even if one really possessed it, could not ensure a steady income or even an income at all. What, he asked again, was the use of genius to a man if he died for want of bread? Only one thing would buy food—money. Let Paul make sure of the future by proving to himself that his painting would pay before he took it up as a career.

All this and more was heard in the Cézanne house in town and in the Jas de Bouffan. Uneasily, Paul pressed his point; he was sufficiently the son of his father to regard with disfavor the idea of starving for his art; his talk of a garret in Paris, put to the test, reduced itself to talk. He hated law, was no more than lukewarm about banking, and was coming to love drawing and painting. He had doubts about his gift, however, which his father, reading his mind, did not lessen. But his mother spoke up for him. Rubens and Veronese, she pointed out, were also named Paul. She claimed a little oddly that this was a sign of destiny. Glad of any support, Paul did not flinch from the compliment. Marie was on his side. Zola wrote letter after fiery letter. The gentle argument went on.

Eventually, in February, 1860, his father beat a skillful retreat; he would agree to Paul trying his hand in Paris, he said, if the master at the Aix Academy supported him. Zola jumped at this as a sign of surrender; prematurely, for the master said that Paul was not yet fit for Paris. Furious, Zola accused him of wishing to keep a pupil. Paul, though disappointed, saw some reason in the man's advice to study the model and draw from plaster casts in the academy to improve his technique.

But Cézanne being what he was, the decision affected his morale. He tried to comfort himself and his friend by counting his blessings: with two loves, "the love of woman and the love of the beautiful" as the basis of his life, what right had he to complain? But he was quite unable to live up to his words. He might love woman, but no woman showed any sign of returning the love. He might love the beautiful expressed through painting, but the master's decision only echoed his own doubts about his ability to express the beauty. He decided that he must try to study law seriously, please his father by taking his degree, then claim as reward a trial in Paris. Meanwhile he began to draw from the model.

His resolve did not last long. The next year, 1860, showed a seesaw of emotions which irritated everyone. First he lost hope of progress at the academy, questioned his talent, spoke of taking up the law in earnest. He asked Zola, how could he speak to his father about Paris and a career as painter when his faith in himself had gone?

This attitude disgusted the brisk and forthright Émile and produced a stream of words from Paris. "You sound depressed in your last letter, you even talk of throwing away your brushes. You bemoan your loneliness. You are bored. Isn't this dreadful boredom the malady of us all? Isn't it the evil of our century? And isn't our discouragement a result of this depression which stifles us. . . . Take up your brushes again, give your imagination free rein. I have faith in you."

"If you were here you would comfort and encourage me," replied Paul wistfully. He was right; letters had not the force of the forceful presence of his friend; they did something, but not enough, and the young Cézanne, hemmed between two strong and contrary influences, the warm protests of Zola and the example of the successful, fond father, managed to make the worst of both worlds. Unable to abandon either, he satisfied neither. For the next stage was inevitable; his resolve to work in earnest at the law collapsed—he could not endure it, and Zola's backing tempted him to neglect it once more; but though he continued to work at the academy he did so without real confidence.

One result of this second stage was a difference with Baille. Émile gone, Baille and Cézanne did not see a great deal of each other, but the memories and the friendship stood unimpaired. Then Baille decided to become an engineer; he was not prepared, he said, "to die in an attic for the sake of glory," and urged Cézanne and Zola to become realistic and find themselves a safe position. He had, in short, come over to the way of thought of Cézanne's father: not objecting to the arts, not relying on them either. Cézanne, who hesitated to speak openly to his father, had not the same scruples with Baille. He dealt shortly with him. Baille complained to Zola, and Cézanne in reply apologized with a "You know very well that with my disposition I'm not always responsible for my actions."

The excuse struck both Zola and Baille as flimsy; they were quite used to the difficult Cézanne; what they could not accept was a display of temperament from a young man who seemed unable to make up his mind about anything, since both in their different ways had decided their future. They were shortsighted; Cézanne's scruples, hesitations, outbreaks bore no relation to his feeling for painting. Both being lesser men than he, they misunderstood him. But Zola at least knew that his friend depended on him for encouragement: he continued to supply it. He did not mince words: "Is painting only a whim," he asked, "which seized you one day when you felt bored? Is it no more than a pastime, a subject to discuss, an excuse for evading the law classes? If so, I understand your behavior; you are right not to force the issue and cause further trouble with your family. But if painting is your vocation—and that's how I have always seen it—if you feel confident of achieving something by painting after working hard at it, then you are an enigma to me, a sphinx, someone indescribably contradictory and obscure. One of two things must be true; either you don't want to be a painter, in which case you are realizing your aim admirably, or you do want to, in which case I don't understand you at all."

Cézanne had used a sentence in his last letter—a very pessimistic one—which puzzled his friend. "I intend to speak in a way that says nothing, for my behavior contradicts my words," he said. This remark explained well enough the dilemma in which he found himself, at one moment bold in speech and irresolute in action, at another quite the reverse—the typical behavior of the man whose true love is obscured by another kind of love, by duty, and by lack of faith in himself.

But to Zola, straightforward, uncomplicated, his words were double Dutch, and he continued with something that he understood, a plain attempt to rouse Paul into some kind of action. "What is your behavior? That of a sluggard, I don't doubt, but what's surprising about that? You are obliged to do work that is distasteful to you and you want to ask your father to let you come to Paris to paint; I can't see any contradiction between your actions and such a request. You neglect the law, you go to the academy or the museum, painting is the only work you find to your liking; in this I find an excellent harmony between your desires and actions. Shall I tell you—but don't get angry—what's the matter with you? You are lacking in character. You dread fatigue of any kind, mental and physical. Your guiding principle is to let things take their course and to leave yourself at the mercy of time and chance. . . . If I were in your place I would risk all to gain all and not float vaguely between such differing futures, the studio and the Bar. I'm sorry for you because you must suffer a lot from your uncertainty, but for me this would only be yet another incentive to tear off the mask. One thing or the other; be a lawyer or be a painter; don't remain a nameless creature wearing a paint-stained toga."

In the end his friend's remonstrances had their effect; they were not facile, as Cézanne knew; if Zola could not really imagine his quandary, not having his feeling for his father or his uncertainty about his own gifts, at least he was risking everything himself—everything except the affection of a parent; his life in Paris was a misery, literature seemed far away, but he persevered cheerfully. So Paul, always impressionable with the few he loved, responded by applying himself to painting and drawing from life with a new enthusiasm.

This led to the third and last stage of the troubled year of 1860. By the time Cézanne registered at the academy in November for the third year running, his mind was, if not made up, more decided than it had ever been; he would paint, he would have nothing to do with the law. He no longer confined himself to the official tuition, but began to paint in the open in his spare time. For the first time he proved his fervor, not by speech or writing but by physical suffering; refusing to wait for the arrival of landscape painters' weather, he spent day after winter day in the country before his easel, painting until his chilled hand would no longer hold the brush.

Zola applauded, and his friend, flushed with courage, again bearded his father. Louis-Auguste was not easily convinced of a real change of heart—the argument went on well into 1861—believing that his son's enthusiasms came more from Zola than from his own convictions. If he had needed evidence Baille could have supplied it, Baille then studying at Marseilles in preparation for the École Polytechnique in Paris. It was from Baille that Zola heard of the banker's belief and to Baille that he defended himself. "Monsieur Cézanne," he wrote, "has seen his son destroy the plans he formed for him. The embryo banker discovers that he is a painter and, sensing that he has grown the wings of an eagle, wants to fly out of the nest. Surprised by this metamorphosis and the desire for liberty, M. Cézanne can't comprehend that painting can be preferred to banking, the open air to his dusty office. He can't understand that God intended these things because God, having created him a banker, created his son a painter. M. Cézanne decided to solve the riddle another way; having examined the question thoroughly, he comes to the conclusion that I am responsible for it, that I made Paul what he is today, that I robbed the bank of its dearest treasure. The words 'bad company' were used, no doubt, and Émile Zola, man of letters, becomes an intriguer, a false friend, and I don't know what besides. It is all the more sad because it is absurd."

This was special pleading. Louis-Auguste was irritated with his son's friend and with some reason. He doubted whether, without Zola, his son would be talking of making a career as painter. Knowing that Paul could not succeed as painter or anything else on a borrowed enthusiasm, he was worried for him and annoyed with his friend's irresponsibility. This doubt, joined to a natural reluctance to see an only son drop out of the business he had built up, made him stubborn. Could he have seen into the future, his attitude might have been different. Could Zola have seen into the future, he would not have tried to excuse himself but would have gloried in the part he played.

Perhaps Louis-Auguste was unwise enough to criticize Zola during the course of the family discussions. Whatever the cause, Paul finally took the bit between his teeth. He did so in his own way. Not for him a penniless dash to Paris, getting lifts from whom he could and scratching a living there as best he could. With his curious blend of the passionate and the cautious he decided that to live in Paris as Émile lived, too poor to do the work he wanted, would be a folly. He was not prepared to starve or to do anything but learn to paint better. If he could not do this, then he would not anger or distress his father by trying to go there.

Feeling thus, his problem was to persuade his father to agree with sufficient good will to provide the money. Argument failing, he applied the means of passive resistance. Louis-Auguste liked to have his family around him, he liked his family to be in harmony. Paul began to stay away from home till all hours. During the short time he was obliged to be in the house he refused to speak a word.

After a few weeks of this his father gave way. He was not a tyrant, he disliked unpleasantness. He believed, too, that a trial of Paris would shake what he still thought to be his son's faint faith. He knew Paul's passion for Aix and its countryside, he knew his love of home. On this he relied. Paul, he said, could go to Paris. And, to show that he had no permanent ill-will for Zola, he accepted without question his estimate of the allowance required for Paul.

Toward the end of April, 1861, they set out. They, because this first venture at Paris was far removed from the solitary journey of the pioneering young Émile three years earlier. The Cézanne home was a united one and Paul, then twenty-two, was not to be allowed to venture into the great city alone and uncared for. With him traveled his father and Marie, his silent but devoted sister. They did not leave him until they saw him established in rooms in Rue Coquillière which were both respectable and clean. They were more than that; whether intended or not, they presented Paul with a daily reminder of his destiny as M. Cézanne read it. The Rue Coquillière ran past the Bourse; every time the would-be painter came out of the house he was faced by that great symbol of high finance.

CHAPTER THREE

Paris Interlude

1861

Louis-Auguste's knowledge of his son was, up to a point, correct and more to be relied on than the son's knowledge of himself. In less than five months Paul was home again and thankful to be there. He liked nothing about Paris except a few of the pictures in the Louvre.

In one sense this Paris interlude was sheer farce. It consisted broadly of one attempt after another of Cézanne to run away and in one attempt after another of Zola to keep him there. More seriously, these five months encouraged the misanthropical attitude in Cézanne which was to dog him for the rest of his life.

His first shock was the change in the relationship between the two friends. At Aix they had been two country boys playing and dreaming romantically of future glory. The glory had been set in Paris because to a French boy Paris is the inevitable Mecca, but it was a Paris never seen on land or sea. When at last they met in Paris, Émile had changed. The country boy had been swallowed by the city. Perhaps his Paris birth predisposed him to the capital, perhaps he was naturally a city-dweller, perhaps he was simply adaptable. Whatever the cause,

33

he had changed, and, from Paul's point of view, changed alarmingly. He welcomed his friend with genuine fervor, he said truly that he had been miserable in Paris, yet to Paul, after a few days, it was clear that Zola disliked only his unsuccess in the city, that the city itself and the life of a city pleased him. Zola had become a Parisian, sitting at the cafés, strolling the river quays, a man of the world. Even his accent had altered; he spoke with the clipped nasal Parisian voice, brisk and businesslike.

Cézanne's first impression of Paris was of a noisy, cold, damp place where people hurried along pavements without good reason, talked when they had nothing to say, were mercenary and unfriendly. He did not change this impression; he was to hold it for life; after Aix he found Paris vulgar, tiring, expensive. Above all, he found it unfriendly. He was not prepared to go to Paris without money: his father had supplied money. He was not prepared to go there without a friend: Zola supplied the friendship. So at least Cézanne, a timid soul in some respects, had calculated. But the old Zola had gone, or disappeared, the moment he set foot outside Aix; in his place was this sophisticated young man who talked twenty to the dozen about literature, no longer a literature in the clouds as when they had speculated and dreamed on the banks of the Arc, but an everyday literature: who was doing this, saying that, whether one could gain an entree to this journal or that. To Cézanne, the idealist, this was not only a falling away; it was the presentation of a side of Zola that he did not recognize and did not wish to know.

But without Zola, the old Zola, Paris was a desert and his position there a mockery. After the first week or two of sight-seeing with his friend he began to drop away; he was too busy, he would say. And he wrote to an acquaintance at the Aix Academy: "I must admit that I am none too cheerful. I fritter my life away in every direction. The Atelier Suisse keeps me busy from six in the morning till eleven. I have a kind of meal for fifteen sous, not very grand, but what can one expect? I am not starving. I thought that by leaving Aix I should leave behind the boredom that dogged me there. In fact all I have done is to change my address and the boredom has followed. I have left behind my parents, my friends, and some habits, that's the whole difference. And to think that I roam about almost all day. I have seen—it is naïve to say so—the Louvre, the Luxembourg, Versailles. You know the boring things housed in these admirable monuments—they are astounding, startling."

He added, "Don't think I am becoming a Parisian"; a precaution which would have struck the puzzled and rather irritated Zola as laughable had it not been so painfully true.

Cézanne's excuse for not seeing more of his friend was his need to work, an unexceptionable reason. He did work but not happily and so not very profitably. He learned, but slowly and at a cost which he thought was far too high—the cost of his dignity and peace of mind. The Paris schools of those days were rough and ready places, the students serious only about their own work and that only for a time, highspirited, rowdy, and with a passion for the practical joke. Cézanne provided the perfect butt; they mocked his provincial clothes, his provincial accent, his sidelong, sullen glances, his style of drawing.

This ragging was, and is, no respecter of persons. All have to go through it. Provincial students offer more obvious targets, but the Paris schools are used to provincials and quickly mold them in their own image. But not Cézanne. Cézanne took a pride in emphasizing his

non-Parisian ancestry; on the few occasions when he
deigned to speak he deepened his Provençal brogue with
mangled vowels, he stood even more awkwardly than
he need, he remained grimly solemn through all witticisms, he refused to be drawn. Disapproval was writ
large all over him. He showed himself self-opinionated,
violently criticizing the precepts of the day. He refused
to draw a line against his principles. He was not alone
in this; most students with a mind of their own set themselves to defy or ridicule the academic, but for the most
part with a certain tact and much humour; Cézanne
went at it like a bull at a gate. In the result they escaped
censure, he never. He was no Gauguin with a manner, no
Van Gogh with an appeal. He had no dignity, no geniality,
no trust. He had the air of one who expected the worst
and he was given the worst.

The Atelier Suisse, nicknamed the "Académie" as a
counterblast to the official Academy, was used by im-
pecunious young painters to draw from the model at
low fees and at almost any hour. Older men worked and
visited there too, and had Cézanne only known, he had
been noticed sympathetically by one of them, Camille
Pissarro, who dropped in from time to time to see a
fellow painter from the West Indies, Francisco Oller.
Pissarro, one of the kindest of men and perceptive too,
did not join in the general ridicule. "Didn't I judge correctly in 1861," he was to write thirty-four years later,
"when Oller and I went to see this peculiar Provençal
in the Atelier Suisse, where Cézanne studies from the
nude were publicly mocked by all the impotents of the
school?" Unhappily, Pissarro did not give his opinion at
the time—he and Cézanne seem not to have spoken to
each other—and the younger man's bitterness and sense
of injustice continued to smolder.

Had Cézanne been a prig as well as appearing a boor, his wretchedness would seem no more than inevitable. In reality he was a dreamer, longing for love and sympathy, a sensitive soul cruelly enwrapped in a manner so unforthcoming that even the most imaginative of men might be pardoned for mistaking it. He believed that his visions, his aims, were shared by many, even by some who tormented him in the school, but he was unable to convey his real feelings to them, unable to convey anything but a defensive approach born of years of self-depreciation, which antagonised all. Yearning for friends, for communion with the like-minded, he could never believe that others would wish to talk, to share with, to love one so crude and unsophisticated and brutish as he. Thinking so, it was so. He was, in truth, not a bad-looking young man; he had fined down and in a dark, undistinguished way was even pleasant to see. But this normality, this chance of mixing with a crowd of students like himself, was thrown away by lack of confidence. He was shunned, made fun of, never once taken seriously. It was a tragedy of uncommunicability. A much greater tragedy than the school years at Aix, where the public ordeal began, because he had hoped to slough his skin in Paris and step out a new man. "I thought I should leave behind the boredom that dogged me there." He wrote "boredom" but meant something quite different. And his "all I have done is to change my address and the boredom has followed" was, had any of them known it, the last *cri de cœur* of the imprisoned. From that moment his future as a solitary settled on him like a garment. From time to time he seemed about to shake it off but always with reservations, always with diminishing effort. At twenty-two the young Cézanne's fate was indicated for life.

2 ～～～～

The fate of the painter was quite another matter. The comedy of the past two years was played out again with Paris as background. Instead of writing his doubts and despair, he now confided them, when he could be got to speak, to Zola in person. Zola was disgusted and hurt. Never before had his personal charm and forcefulness failed to pull Paul into at least a temporary optimism; now, in Paris of all places, and to his face, Cézanne was talking of abandoning painting, returning to Aix, going into the bank—all the dreary round of the letters long before. And this no more than a month after his arrival.

Sometimes he was difficult to get hold of at all, and Zola, who had his fair share of vanity, unloaded some of his chagrin onto Baille—a significant choice. He rarely saw Cézanne, he said; when his friend had finished sketching and painting he usually ate and went straight to bed. "Is this the kind of thing I'd hoped for?" he demanded rhetorically.

He gave a résumé, colored by irritation but fundamentally true, of the Paris Cézanne: "Paul is still the same fine but odd chap I knew at school. As evidence that he has lost none of his originality I need only tell you that he had no sooner got here than he talked of going back to Aix. To have fought for three years for this trip and now not to care a straw for it! In the face of such a character and such impulsive and unreasoning changes of behavior I confess that I retire to my logic and say nothing. To prove something to Cézanne would be like trying to persuade the spires of Notre Dame to dance a quadrille; he might say yes, but he wouldn't

budge an inch. And note that the years have developed
his obstinacy without giving rational grounds for it. He
is all of a piece, inflexible, unmoldable; nothing moves
him, nothing can force him to make a concession. He
doesn't even want to discuss what he thinks; he hates
a discussion because he finds talk tiring and because
he would have to change his opinion if his opponent were
in the right. So there you have him, cast into the center
of life but bringing with him certain ideas which he's
unwilling to alter on any judgment but his own. Yet he's
the nicest fellow in the world, always agreeing with one—
the result of his aversion to argument."

This was far from the whole truth about Cézanne, and
Zola soon went on to qualify his picture: "If he happens
to put forward an opinion contrary to yours and you
question it, he flies into a rage without wishing to examine what you say, shouts that you know nothing about
the subject, and jumps on to something else. If you
persist in arguing—what am I saying?—if you simply
talk with a man of this kind, you won't make an inch
of headway but you will have seen a very queer personality. I had hoped that time would have changed him
a bit but he's just as I left him. My plan of behavior
is therefore very simple: never to interfere with his
whims, to give him at most very indirect advice, to throw
myself on his good nature as far as the continuation of
our friendship is concerned."

This was more a pious hope than a plan of campaign;
Zola was no more able to efface himself than his friend
was able to listen to another man's reason. But the genuine
feeling between the two of them remained. Cézanne
needed the thought of Zola even when he could do without him in person, and Zola, even when trying to ration-

alize his friend's emotional and instinctive reaction to
everything, felt sure that his illogical, intolerant approach
to life was a sure sign of latent genius.

So there was trouble but no break, weeks of intimacy
followed by weeks of virtual separation, with Cézanne
working morning and evening at the Académie Suisse
and in the afternoons in the studio of Villevieille. This
young man, one of the elder students in the Aix academy,
had moved to Paris and offered room to Cézanne to
work; offered advice, too, which Paul for the most part
rejected. There were very awkward moments. Villevieille,
like Zola, put Cézanne down as plain obstinate, but he,
like Zola, was mistaken, misled by Cézanne's brusque
manner and inability to explain himself. Cézanne was
obstinate but with a purpose. He had seen in the academy
at Aix how one student after another had allowed his
personal vision to be clouded by the official pressure to
conform to academic standards. Villevieille, typical example of the conformist, was producing work in Paris
from which all personality had been expunged; he was
like a hundred other competent painters, and his advice
to Paul was, in effect, to join the throng. Paul declined,
ungraciously because he knew no better way of declining;
he would not move an inch from his chosen path; he
would find himself in his own fashion or abandon the
search. He believed in his special vision as painter, unclear though it was: that or nothing, he said. To Villevieille, as to Zola, this seemed highhanded, coming from
an inexperienced young man. It was. It was also admirable, which they did not see, that their friend should
fight for the purity of his "sensation." His refusal to be
guided made the fight a long and hurtful one, hurtful
to him and to those who tried to help. The future was

to prove him right; the present was almost all wretched-ness.

So Cézanne remained incalculable; Zola, after he had relieved his mind, remained the good friend trying to save not so much a sinking ship as one which insisted on putting back to harbor. The shifts Zola was put to to keep Cézanne in Paris were laughable, as he was the first to see after his irritation had passed. By the middle of June he was telling Baille with a despair not wholly mock: "Cézanne has many fits of discouragement; despite his somewhat overdone scorn of fame I can see that he would like to win it. When he works badly he talks of nothing less than a return to Aix and going into an office as a clerk. Then I have to read him long lectures on the folly of going back. He agrees readily and gets on with his work. All the same he is possessed by this idea; twice already he has been on the verge of leaving; I'm afraid he may escape me at any moment."

Not long after this, Zola called at the rooms of Cézanne, who had been laying low in rather a suspicious manner. Sure enough, he found trunks packed and his friend on the point of departure. Wisely, he did not remonstrate. He simply reminded Cézanne that he had promised to make his portrait.

This portrait—one of many that Cézanne was to make of him—led straight to another would-be flight. He began twice, remained dissatisfied and asked Zola for a third sitting. Arrived for the sitting, Zola discovered the trunks on the floor again and his friend rapidly filling them from the wardrobe and chest of drawers—piling them in any-how and with a face expressing the utmost despair.

"I'm leaving tomorrow," he announced.

"And what about my portrait?" asked Zola.

"I've just destroyed it," replied Cézanne. "I tried to re-touch it this morning but as it only got worse and worse I destroyed it. So I'm going."

Zola with considerable self-command simply asked the afflicted young man to lunch. He stayed with him all day and had his reward; before going back to his rooms Cézanne promised to stay in Paris.

But this kind of thing wore the nerves and patience. "That's merely a delaying action," Zola told Baille, who was himself coming to Paris in the autumn and who had already been instructed to hold out this arrival in his letters to Cézanne as a bait. "If he doesn't go this week, he'll go next. You can expect to hear that he's gone any day. I even think he might do well to go. Paul may have the genius of a great painter but he'll never have the genius to become one. The least obstacle makes him despair."

Zola's impatience was understandable, yet Cézanne had his point of view, too. He had come to Paris expecting a personal miracle; the miracle had not happened. He had come to Paris hoping that his gift would be recognized and developed as it could not be in the academy at Aix; this too did not happen. All that had happened was that he and his work were rejected in the most hurtful way, by ridicule. That he might be his own worst enemy occurred to him seldom and merely added to despondency; at other times the beginnings of a persecution mania were already stirring in him. But from his point of view, why stay in Paris? He did not like it or the life led in it, he was spending money (a great point in his father's son), living badly and learning little. And, final, inevitable conclusion, was there any purpose in learning this little? If he could not be a great painter he would not be a little one. Rather the bank than that.

His admiration for his father was never far out of his mind. His father had prophesied that what had come to pass would come to pass. Try Paris, he had said in effect, but I don't believe you are a painter, I believe you are a banker; your heart is in Aix and will be in the bank there. Was not this mature wisdom? After a few months of Paris and despite all that Zola could say or do, Paul silently capitulated. Zola had with great difficulty extracted a promise that he would not leave before the autumn. Cézanne kept his promise to the letter; on the earliest possible day of autumn he returned to Aix and announced that he was ready to go into the bank.

CHAPTER FOUR

End of a Banker
1861–1863

MONSIEUR CÉZANNE's triumph had a short life. His son entered the bank voluntarily but had not been in it more than a few weeks before he wanted to leave it. A brief spell of office work made even the Académie Suisse seem like a dream of freedom. In November he again enrolled at the academy in Aix, and followed this hint to his father with others, covering with drawings and verses the pages of the ledger he was supposed to make entries into. One of his couplets read:

Cézanne le banquier ne voit pas sans frémir
Derrière son comptoir naître un peintre à venir.

Early the next year Monsieur Cézanne took the hint. Always practical, he realized that Paul would never become a businessman; and as he had no wish to make one of his children wretched or to foist on the bank an inefficient clerk, he abandoned the twenty-year-old dream of a successor. No more was heard in the Cézanne home of Paul's duty. His father mastered his disappointment well, his mother and sister (the younger girl, Rose, was only a child of seven) already favored a career as painter. It was, however, understood that Paul would really give

44

his mind to his work and that when he went to Paris
again, as everyone realized that he must, he would overcome unpleasantnesses and make the most of his time
and the money spent on him. And it is a proof of the
stirring of genius that he, with none but unhappy memories of Paris, hating to pledge himself and still unsure
of his gift, kept to his side of the bargain. He worked
hard and with a kind of desperate intensity. The atmosphere of the academy helped his morale; after the
Académie Suisse it appeared, if behind the times, at least
tolerably friendly; he was somebody there, a recognized
if not specially popular person. At the worst he was left
alone; at best he found an acquaintance or two to come
out sketching and painting in that loved stretch of
country between the town, the dam, and the Sainte-
Victoire.

He quickly passed on the news of his release to Zola
and bridged a letterless gap. Zola had heard of the retreat to the bank with disgust and anger; he did not
write, nor did Cézanne, who knew well enough what his
friend thought of him. But Zola responded warmly and,
when he and Baille came down in the summer, began
once more to take Paul under his wing as far as that
stubborn man permitted. Plans for Paris abounded. But
the summer differed greatly from earlier ones. They
walked as usual, bathed in river and reservoir, talked,
but lighthearted confidence had disappeared and their
unity had to lean hard on past glories. Zola had known
what it was to go hungry and to work at a menial job;
though he had begun to write the inevitable autobiographical first novel he had less to say about a brilliant
future in literature; he had come to realize that, since
man has to eat, a penniless author would have to start
at the bottom; and the bottom was journalism. Baille,

then a student at the École Polytechnique, was determined to make a success of himself as an engineer and gave short shrift to the old idea of the poet or painter dying in an attic to ensure posthumous glory; he did not encourage the higher flights of imagination. Cézanne, always the quietest in more youthful days except for the occasional burst of high spirits or anger, had sobered still further; there was no looking back and he knew it. So the era of dreams had passed; no longer did Zola declare, "I love the idea of poverty," or talk blithely of "nourishing himself on great thoughts." All was practical. Ambitious, too, however; Zola confident of eventual fame, Cézanne fumblingly nerving himself to his destiny —a destiny that he at once longed for and feared.

He proved, soon after his friends' return to Paris, that his own apparently disastrous visit there had borne fruit; displaying a self-knowledge unusual in a young man of twenty-three, he told Zola that although he would and must return to the schools in Paris he did not plan to work in the north as almost every painter did; he intended to return regularly to Aix and expected to remain a southern painter. He did not then use the phrase *"ma petite sensation"*—that was to come much later—but even at this early stage he had begun to believe instinctively that he would find his unique sensation, his true expression of himself, in depicting the southern scenery and people he loved so well. How original such a decision was, he perhaps suspected; for in Paris it was customary to dismiss the strong light of the south as an enemy to the painter, taking the color out of the landscape and destroying the mystery of atmosphere which was just then beginning its rise to popularity.

In November he returned to Paris. His father, having accepted the inevitability of Paul as painter, reacted characteristically. If he insisted on becoming a painter it was only common sense, he pointed out, to make himself successful. And he knew enough about painting to know that the road to success led through the École des Beaux-Arts. That, therefore, must be Paul's goal. And it was on this understanding that Cézanne left Aix for the second time. He went back for the moment to the Académie Suisse only because, his father believed, he had to pass an examination before being admitted to the École.

Two months later, in January, 1863, his father combined business and duty in a visit to the Bourse by making sure that his son intended to take the examination and was working for it. He was working for it, though not with enthusiasm—a lack which his father did not perceive but which the examiners did. He failed.

2 ~~~~

When Monsieur Cézanne advised Paul to enter the Beaux-Arts he was typifying the attitude of the wealthy bourgeoisie in France, the new patrons of art since the falling away of the old, the aristocracy and the state. He was precisely the kind of man who would buy paintings to decorate his house and impress his neighbors; having no knowledge of painting but, he believed, carrying his business acumen into art, he thought that he could only be sure of a good bargain if he bought from a qualified painter. And in the short view this was true. A qualified painter, in the eyes of the bourgeois patron, was one who had been given the seal of official approval. This approval could be gained in one way only, by a course of tuition at the Beaux-Arts, whose teachers were selected by the Academy of Fine Arts and which also nominated the jury who selected works to be shown at the Salon. And as the Salon was the sole recognized means of showing one's wares to the public, the only painters to make a name and money were those who had been approved pupils of the Beaux-Arts.

The career of a successful painter did not vary in essentials from the career of a successful politician; he had to have the right training, know the right people, and show the right kind of canvas at the Salon. The merit of his work consisted entirely in the extent of his adherence to principles laid down by the Academy and taught at the Beaux-Arts. This restriction on the freedom of painters might have been less harmful had the academic principles been in any degree fluid. As it was, they had not moved an inch since the time of David, half a century earlier. They were based on the assumption that to draw correctly was more important than to paint well: line before color, classicism before romanticism was the slogan of Ingres, the power behind the Academy. This understood, official approval was given primarily to paintings dealing with what were considered noble themes— the reconstruction of a classical tale, patriotic battle scenes, great moments in history. The Salon jury also looked with a kind eye on the unimpeachable nude which, being lifeless, could not offend bourgeois susceptibilities, and on every sort of pretty picture—children playing with pets, mothers and babies, posies of rigid flowers, sentimentalized versions of the peasant at work in the fields or taking his ease in his rose-covered cottage. Above all, the painter was expected to meet the widespread need for a story; his picture had to be not only explanatory to the last degree but preferably carry a title which would either whet curiosity, provide dialogue, or doubly underline his meaning.

These appeals to a lazy eye, a sentimental mind, a crude patriotism, a conventional religious sense, an adolescent love of narrative were exactly suited to purchasers who knew nothing of painting, were without taste but had plenty of money. The men who had made quick fortunes in the industrial revolution, the new rulers of France, were anxious to spend their gains in a manner which would impress, yet, being hard-headed, they demanded value for money. Pictures bought at the biennial Salon met both aims admirably; they made a lavish show in the new houses the bourgeoisie were building and, bought from painters officially approved and often enough with a medal or decoration, could confidently be expected to prove an excellent investment. The purchaser had no need to trust his own eye or judgment; he could rely on the Salon jury. And if even then he remained uncertain which masterpiece to buy, the critics would tell him; for they, with an eye on their livelihood, almost to a man paid lip service to academic taste. The typical Salon product had the final merit of looking expensive; it was glossly efficient, proclaiming in every line, every careful brush stroke, the recognized center of manufacture. It guaranteed also the freedom from genuine emotion which its buyer either could not or did not want to feel. Pleasure without pain—that was the aim of official art. And it was as such an official painter, successful, decorated, and eventually achieving the ultimate honor of a seat in the Academy, that Louis-Auguste inevitably saw his son.

3 〰️

In a country with the great tradition of France, the official attitude to painting naturally met opposition.

Most of this came, as would be expected, from the
hundreds of painters not good enough technically or
mentally even to find a place in the existing Salon. But
there was also worthy opposition. In the painters it came
from Delacroix, Courbet and a young man who was just
being talked about by the avant-garde when Cézanne
first came up to Paris—Edouard Manet. Among the critics,
opposition was headed by Baudelaire and, a long way
behind in stature, the fiery Zacharie Astruc, admirer of
Manet, and the revolutionary Edmond Duranty.

This opposition, though vocal, had little power. Delacroix had become famous, Courbet well known, and that
was all. And for the young men who drew beside Cézanne
at the Académie Suisse, as for all serious young painters,
the outlook was poor. There were not then, as now, a
dozen or more private galleries which could be persuaded or paid to arrange shows which the public would
visit and the press review. If these painters could not get
their work into the Salon, their only chance of selling,
an occasional personal contact excepted, rested in the
efforts of their paint dealer in his shop or in the stag-
ing of a one-man exhibition, a costly affair far beyond
their means and which the critics would be unlikely to
visit. And the only way they could win a sympathetic
hearing from the selection committee of the Salon was
by prostituting their view of art.

At that time the remedy seemed to all to lie in the
opening of the Salon to all good and original work—in
other words, in a drastic overhaul of the jury who choose
the pictures. Most young painters were simple enough to
think that their work had only to be prominently displayed to be appreciated and sold. This natural thought
was held by Cézanne. The idea that the potential buyer
had to be educated to good painting was long in coming,

though Zola, who relinquished a tenet almost as easily as his friend clung to it, was to be one of the pioneers.

When Cézanne arrived in Paris for the second time, the Académie Suisse buzzed with talk about the 1863 Salon, to be held as usual in May. Possibly because Pissarro had commented favorably on his work to some who worked at the Académie, possibly because Cézanne, having taken the plunge in earnest, became a little more approachable, he made friends with one or two young men, chief of whom were Antoine Guillemet and Armand Guillaumin. The first of these had a mediocre talent and is known today, heavily mustached and rather shinily plump in his frock coat, as the male sitter with Berthe Morisot in Manet's *Le Balcon*. Guillaumin was another matter; a young clerk in a government office, he spent every available moment at his easel. Encouraged by Pissarro, he was showing signs of genuine talent and, encouraged by Pissarro or not, he had the wit to see that in Cézanne the Académie Suisse possessed not simply a rustic character of more strangeness than charm, but an original artist. The hallmark of the great painter at every stage of his career is a refusal to be anything but himself; he will not conform to convention because he cannot. The drawings of Cézanne at the Académie, the work which roused such laughter, were imperfect, were a mere approximation of the mature artist, because he lacked self-knowledge and technical skill; nevertheless they had, to the seeing eye, a quality which raised them above the correct, conforming work all round him; in their primitive force they betrayed his Italian ancestry, in their hint of passion they pointed to the original artist.

Guillaumin, observing something of this, became friendly with Cézanne, introduced him to Pissarro, with whom he used to paint on weekends, and encouraged him to submit work to the Salon of 1863. He was doing likewise. Neither could have had much hope of being accepted, but with youthful enthusiasm they painted on.

Their work was not accepted. Nor was the work of hundreds of other painters; more than four thousand canvases were rejected by the jury of official painters. This wholesale slaughter, far greater than ever before, accomplished what years of agitation by the unofficial painters had never been able to do; appalled, even some of the official critics murmured, the great body of painters were mutinous, the press took it up. The agitation penetrated court circles. Louis Napoleon, no judge of art, thought in terms of politics; within the bounds of what he considered to be safety he was anxious to win the regard of the intelligent by posing as an art lover in the widest possible sense. He decided that, if their owners agreed, the rejected works should be shown in a separate exhibition in the same building as the official salon. This exhibition, the famous Salon des Refusés, opened in the middle of May. Cézanne's work was there, and Guillaumin's, together with canvases by Manet, Pissarro and many others.

The gesture failed. Louis Napoleon was given to the making of liberal motions which alarmed him so much that he immediately nullified them by acts of extreme reaction. He had a gift for pleasing none. He did so here. Worried by the anger of the official school of painters headed by the Academy, he made a point of declaring his personal sympathy; he bought the most popular painting in the Salon, an efficient but characterless *Birth of Venus*, granted the painter, Cabanel, promotion in the Legion of Honor, and approved his election to the Institute, the reactionary body of which the Academy was a part. At the same time he publicly expressed his dislike for the most talked-of painting in the Salon des Refusés, Manet's

Le Dejeuner sur l'herbe: "Immodest," he said, reprovingly.

These gestures, though tactical, rightly represented the Emperor's views on painting. They struck a blow at the modern painters he was supposed to be offering a fair chance of judgment by the public. But even had he kept silent their fate at this exhibition could scarcely have been otherwise. The public was not educated beyond an appreciation of the obvious; common prejudice was skilfully played on by a section of the popular press mobilized by the official artists.

The result was an example of crowd hysteria scandalous even in an age of bourgeois bad manners. The Salon des Refusés was turned into a joke by most of the critics and by the thousands of people who struggled to get in day after day. "The fools . . . rain down here by the million and scoff outrageously at everything." And a neutral critic, an Englishman, complained that owing to the crowd's attitude it was impossible to judge any of the paintings fairly because impossible to approach them in a serious state of mind: "The threshold once past, the gravest visitor burst into peals of laughter."

This demonstration of mass philistinism—a demonstration recurring through the ages, as any visitor to the Picasso-Matisse exhibition in London after the war will recall—was, as always, aroused by fear of the unknown. And, as always, it demanded a victim. Cézanne and Guillaumin were ignored, Pissarro let off with a warning. Crowd and critics alike fell on Manet. He, the alarmed public decided, was the bête noire, the ring-leader of the revolutionaries; destroy him and art would relax into safe obscurity. Execration was poured on his *Déjeuner sur l'herbe* (then entitled *Le Bain*) and all the choicest witticisms were reserved for this picture. Although the subject of the painting—a nude woman picnicking with clothed men—was little more than a copy of a Giorgione which respond unanathematized in the Louvre, the public, following Louis Napoleon, found it immodest. So at least they thought. What really disturbed them was Manet's introduction of modern dress. Had the men been dressed, as Giorgione's, in bygone fashions, Manet might have escaped as the author of a period piece; his realism shocked ninety-nine visitors in the hundred; the idea that art had anything to do with the present day, that it was anything but another innocuous decoration, had to be fought and destroyed.

Manet's realism was, in fact, conveyed in more subtle ways, by the unusual use of color contrasts, by his penchant for broad tones, his refusal to cross every T with the brush, the general air of brutally disregarding the careful conventions of the Beaux-Arts. And it was this which elevated him, after the farcical Salon des Refusés had come to an end, into the progressive painters' white hope. Two years earlier, after Manet's *Spanish Guitar Player* had been shown at the Salon, he had been acclaimed by a small band of "moderns" as the begetter of a "strange, new" method of painting, and had become the friend and favorite of Baudelaire, Astruc, and Duranty. Now he leaped into the leadership of all who detested the stranglehold of the Academy working through the Beaux-Arts. On the death of Delacroix soon afterward, he was painted by Fantin-Latour in his *Hommage à Delacroix* in the center of the master's admirers, the obvious heir; and Guillaumin, Zola, and Cézanne all followed the rest in general admiration. They did not then aspire to meet Manet; although no more than seven years older than Cézanne, he moved in a world of which they only touched the fringe; but they examined his work with reverence and excitement.

Zola and Cézanne's "great discussions" after regular
visits to the Salon des Refusés chiefly concerned the work
of Manet. Zola, longing for a hero to defend as passionately as he sought a profitable fight, found in Manet the
ideal subject. How deeply he understood the painter is
another matter; a born reformer, he was overcome by the
desire to force the world to acknowledge the new painting
as the first stage in the general triumph of realism. He
was admirably equipped for the task: he wrote hard-
hitting prose, filled with conviction, he had infinite courage and all the insensitiveness of the journalist. Controversy was meat and drink to him. Up to then his
misfortune had been to lack a purpose to be controversial
about. The time to "make" Cézanne was obviously not
yet; his friend's talent remained unclear. Then came the
Salon des Refusés and Zola's way shone bright. That, he
told himself, was his life's work. He was young and head-
strong; he was mistaken, it was not his life's work, merely
a forerunner of it. But his sense of timing was good; his
championship of Manet and the new painting was to make
his own name.

The "great discussions" were nine-tenths Zola. And not
simple because Zola commonly did most of the talking:
Cézanne's view of Manet was by no means so definite as
his friend's. Zola, whatever he might say, was looking primarily for a reason for enthusiasm; the fact that it happened to be a painter was sheer chance. Cézanne was
looking for something much more difficult to find; his
raison d'être as painter. He wanted to paint, that alone
was definite; what and how to paint remained mysteries.
He suspected that the answer to the first would be found
in the south; the answer to the second would as certainly
be supplied by Paris. Manet was the first modern painter
to touch him, yet it is doubtful whether he ever whole-

heartedly approved of Manet's work. The economy, the strength and the color sense—these aspects of Manet he admired because they were to be primary aspects of his own work. But he could not like the lack of taste in subject and treatment that Manet was so often to show, a lack of which the younger man was almost incapable.

So, though subscribing to the avant-garde admiration of Manet, he did not, as so many others, slavishly copy the new master. On the contrary, the most noticeable influence of this time was Delacroix, whose death drove Cézanne to join the copyists in the Louvre. Like others— Van Gogh, for example—he fell in love with the bold and unusual colors of Delacroix, his green, blue, purple. Like others too, and not so happily, he was influenced by the large group compositions, a type of work which in other hands could too easily fall into the grandiose. This last was to delay the emergence of the true Cézanne.

CHAPTER FIVE

The Painter Appears
1863–1866

For the next four years Cézanne alternated between
Paris and Aix. Broadly speaking, he was learning to
paint in Paris and applying the result of his learning
in his native town. He even rejoined the local academy.

From this period date the first canvases which could be
described a little laxly as the true Cézanne—the portraits
of his mother's brother Dominic, of his father, his sisters,
and academy and café acquaintances, chiefly the Jewish
poet and local art critic Antoine Valabrègue. These were
done for the most part at the Jas de Bouffan where he had
space and quiet; he spent much of his time there alone
and not only painted his portraits but decorated the salon
with murals.

He was still far from discovering himself. He did not
ever realize that the portraits pointed some part of the
way to his unique "sensation." He was preoccupied by
what seemed to be the primary need to express his imagination. Portrait painting had a bad name inasmuch as
it was done by every painter and many who were not
painters at all; and Cézanne naturally but mistakenly
tended to underrate the imaginative effort involved. Like
so many who found expression difficult by word of mouth,

he lived much of his life in the imagination; there his passionate and idealistic nature sought release. And as soon as his technical ability as painter seemed sufficient, he began to try to say on canvas what was beyond him in speech.

It was at this point that the example of Delacroix proved harmful. Delacroix's imagination worked on a known theme, usually historical. Cézanne tried to paint imaginary scenes on large canvases. In every way this was a mistake. He was technically not up to the handling of such themes, they were in any case fundamentally opposed to his natural genius, and, not least important, his imagination, too often obsessed by sex, turned morbid. Subject and treatment both failed, but obstinate as ever he worked on, devoting to these canvases an amount of time and labor out of proportion to their value.

The portraits, on the other hand, which he painted quickly, bear an immediate resemblance to the mature Cézanne; the strong color, the simplicity and seriousness of handling, the excellent sense of proportion and form. The one considerable difference between this and his great work of the future lay in a general lack of discipline; these were the paintings of a young and passionate man, glorying in vivid color, laying the paint on thickly, somewhat after the manner of Vincent van Gogh twenty years later. Still more characteristic are the still lives, that staple fare of the artist reluctant or unable to pay model fees and, in Cézanne's case, unable to endure the restlessness and light chatter of the cheaper model. Cézanne's fruit is rough-hewn, rocklike, as if he had penetrated to the very core; the solidity is of the nature of his beloved Sainte-Victoire, the color warm and true. Freed from the human element which tended at that time to unbalance him, these still lives were a broad hint of the future, a hint which Cézanne in his humility failed to see. However, work and labor though he might at his imaginary compositions, his peasant caution and good sense prevailed over romanticism when he came to choose work to submit to the Salon.

For he was still sending work to the Salon. "One should always present something to the jury if only to put it in the wrong," he declared. The Salon des Refusés had not been held again, so the Salon remained "the only battlefield on which an artist could reveal himself." He was rejected in 1864, rejected in 1865, and was preparing submissions for 1866 which, he told Pissarro, "would make the Institute blush with rage and despair"—a natural and forgivable exaggeration.

Before this Salon was held, in January, history was made by the arrival in Aix of Guillemet, seduced by Cézanne's descriptions of this untouched field in painting. Cézanne remained as unpolished as ever; Paris and the Académie Suisse could not break down his strange mixture of shyness, diffidence, and brutal honesty; it actually intensified the revealing physical reaction which made him wince and start away when anyone accidentally touched him. But he had come out of his shell to a degree that astonished the acquaintances at Aix. "He has changed," Valabrègue told Zola; "he speaks."

After a month he and Guillemet returned to Paris and to a Zola become notorious overnight. For some time he had been making money—he was on the staff of the Librairie Hachette—but his first emergence into the limelight came with the publication of his maiden novel, *La Confession de Claude*, at the end of 1865. This book, dedicated to Cézanne and Baille, was the autobiographical romance he had been pondering three years earlier and which contained many references to the carefree summers

at Aix. Mingled with the romance, however, was a good
deal of the later Zola; what Manet was doing in painting
he was trying to do in literature, to put it back onto a
realistic basis. Actually, he was for the most part youth-
fully crude, but he managed to shock the critics successfully enough to lose his job and make a name as the most
daring writer of the day. His reward came quickly; he was
appointed literary editor of *L'Événement*.

Cézanne therefore found him flourishing and, sure sign
of it, holding a weekly salon every Thursday in his rooms.
There came Pissaro when in Paris, a genial, burly, bearded
figure with whom even the captious Cézanne could find
no fault, Baille, Guillemet, Guillaumin, and the sculptor
Philippe Solari from Aix. Cézanne and Solari went well together because the sculptor never made a provocative remark; indeed, this sweet-tempered little man with the face
of a gnome and the eyes of a saint was a dreamer, with his
head so far in the clouds that he gave Cézanne the rare
and agreeable sensation of holding all the conversational
trumps. For the rest, Cézanne usually listened from a
corner, exploding occasionally when the talk riled him
unbearably, but commonly smoking with his customarily
closed intensity, black brows knitted below a forehead
already lengthening as his fine hair fell away, small piercing eyes on the ground. The discussions, when not merely
personal—the latest conquest of the heart, the latest
aspiration—always tended to come back to the theme interesting them all, the progress of realism in art. All
professed to be rescuing art from the romantic and unreal slough into which it had fallen. All, led by Pissarro,
a rabid socialist, wanted bring art back to the common
man. They panted for truth; art should not only be available for the common man but instantly recognizable by
him as true to life; Zola intended to speak plainly in his

criticism, to call a spade a spade in the books he was
meditating; the painters spoke, vaguely but passionately,
of following Manet.

For Manet, passing through yet another martyrdom,
had become even more of an idol to the young painters.
The Salon jury of the previous year, yielding perhaps
to a momentary aberration or influenced by Manet's growing following, had accepted his *Olympia,* the picture of
a nude woman lying on a bed attended by a negress. The
scenes of the Salon des Réfuses were repeated, laughing
crowds jammed before the canvas day after day. The
critics attacked his vulgarity, even Courbet, a professed
realist, turned against him. Once again subject and treatment combined to frighten almost all and their fear was
expressed by abuse. But Manet was made famous—
"better known than Garibaldi" said Degas laughingly at
the Café de Bade—and could do no wrong in the eyes of
the avant-garde of the Paris schools.

At the Café de Bade he held court, sitting on the ter-
race most days as soon as darkness had fallen and painting
was no longer possible. And there, whenever he could
pluck up courage, came Cézanne. For he had at last met
Manet. Soon after his return from Aix, Guillemet showed
Manet some still lives by Cézanne. Manet found them
"powerfully treated," Valabrègue reported at second-
hand. He continued: "Cézanne is very happy about this
though he doesn't expatiate about his happiness or insist
on it as he usually does. Manet is going to call on him.
Parallel temperaments, they will surely understand one
another."

This hope was wildly far from the mark as was the
analysis of temperament. Manet and Cézanne were alike
in this, that both had been brought up in well-to-do
homes and knew little about the struggle to live that

most of their painter friends had to endure. Both were egoists, both in their very different ways dictatorial and both, again for very different reasons, self-opionated. That said, they were poles apart. Manet was bourgeois to the core, Cézanne a peasant with a bourgeois covering; Manet wore his education with an air, Cézanne with a scowl; Manet was fundamentally cold, Cézanne passionate.

However, the great man had noticed Cézanne. He had in fact added to Guillemet a few words which robbed his compliment of all value; Cézanne, he said, "was not much more than an interesting colorist." This remark, which Guillemet of course did not pass on, showed that the master had his blind spots. Even by 1866 Cézanne's portraits and still lives displayed a highly original mind and an eye which saw beyond surface appearances. But Manet was a vain man and had the defect of vanity, an otherwise surprising obtuseness; himself no deliberate rebel, but pushed into the forefront by chance, he had neither the wish nor the knowledge to see rebellion in another form.

But he had spoken favorably, and Cézanne innocently called and was invited to the Café de Bade whenever he was inclined. He was not often inclined. And when he did drag himself to the ordeal and sat well to the rear of the worshippers, he was not only ill at ease but soon actively disapproving. Up to a point his sensations in public can be shared by all who, like him, are unblessed with a social manner or quick tongue and whose emotions run deep. He felt acutely uncomfortable. But this embarrassment was to be crowded out by another feeling. Manet was not only the hero, but acted like one. Too much so, Cézanne thought, critically watching. As he had suspected from Manet's pictures, the man on closer acquaintance revealed a tinge of vulgarity; his handsome, brown-bearded face was a shade coarse, his dandyish clothes were worn a shade too flashily, and his repartee, though clever, could also be merely cheap. For Manet had a reputation for the bon mot which he lived up to to the point of downright rudeness. If his sayings were questioned he was apt to fly into a rage; intolerant of other opinions, he would shout or laugh them down. The law of his gatherings was clearly defined: those present could laugh with but never against him. Only Degas, truly and devastatingly witty, and the formidable Duranty were allowed, with poor grace, to win a verbal battle; the rest were there to listen and applaud. And there was much to hear and much to applaud—the perfection of Manet's technique and the soundness of most of his views were not to be denied, and his ardent championship of the young and adventurous painters warmed all hearts. Or almost all; for the silent Cézanne, so ready to discover a flaw in himself as in others, beady black eyes shooting secret glances at the vivacious central figure, came to have his doubts: was it possible that profound revolution could come from such a man, could the truth be found in such a milieu?

The thoughts turned over and over in the mind of this "strange Provençal" who was trying, single-mindedly and with what silent struggles none can know, to force a path to the painting of the future.

2 ⤳

For the moment, happy to have been recognized by Manet, though with typical reservations forming like a cloud behind the happiness, Cézanne was affected in another direction by the master. The reception given to

Olympia had stiffened the attitude of the jury for 1866:
they threw out every painting possessing the slightest
suspicion of modernity. Sparing of money, Cézanne either
carried his paintings on his back or, as in this case,
trundled them around on a cart, just before closing
time, and exhibited them sardonically to the crowd
gathered outside the door to watch canvases being carried
in. His offerings were rejected and not silently. His most
promising entry was the portrait of Valabrègue, a powerful if crudely painted piece of work with color strongly
and originally applied. The subject of the painting,
recently come to Paris, passed on the news to Aix: "A
philistine in the jury exclaimed on seeing my portrait that
it was not only painted with a knife but with a pistol"—
a more farseeing remark, if applied to Cézanne as painter,
than the man could have dreamed. Only one member of
the jury, Daubigny, spoke up for Cézanne: "He declared
that he preferred pictures brimming over with daring to
the nullities which appear at every Salon." But "he didn't
succeed in convincing them."

Cézanne declared far and wide, before and after each
Salon, that he not only did not expect to be accepted, he
did not wish to be. This was mere self-protection, natural
but misleading, as he showed as soon as his 1866 rejection as made known. Far from rejoicing, he wrote an
angry letter to the Director of Fine Arts insisting that
a Salon des Refusés be reinstituted. And, having no
answer, he wrote again. "Recently I had the honor of
writing to you about my two canvases which the jury
rejected. As you have not replied yet, I feel it my duty
to stress the reasons which made me write you. However,
as you have certainly received my letter there is no need
for me to repeat here the arguments which I thought
necessary to put before you. I content myself with tell-

ing you again that I cannot accept the unauthorized verdict of fellow painters whom I have not given the authority to judge me.

"I write to you, then, to press my request. I wish to appeal to the people and to be shown in spite of any previous rejection. My request does not seem exorbitant to me, and if you asked the painters in my position, all would reply that they repudiate the Jury and that they want to take part in one way or another in an exhibition open to all serious workers. So let the Salon des Refusés be re-established. Even if I were to be the only exhibitor, I wish passionately that the public shall at least know that I don't want to be connected with the gentlemen of the Jury any more, it appears, than they want to be connected with me. I hope, Monsieur, that you will not keep silent any longer. It seems to me that every decent letter deserves a reply."

He had a reply, but not one to satisfy him. The sense of it was given in a scribbled note on his letter: "What he asks is impossible. It is well known that the Salon des Refusés proved unseemly for the dignity of Art and it won't be re-established." That a protest from Cézanne would be listened to was, of course, out of the question; if known at all, he was written off as a follower of Manet: he had never sold a picture and his work was dismissed as the ravings of a so-called young realist who, unable even to go through the Beaux-Arts, hid incompetence under abuse of the successful and a determination to be different for the sake of it. His letters were, however, timed to influence official opinion at the moment when Zola was trying to influence public opinion. For Zola was writing a series of articles in *Le Figaro*, hard-hitting stuff which revealed the scandals of selection by the jury, praised Manet as the pride of modern painting, and tore the Salon exhibits to shreds. He hoped, without much hope, that even the unknown Cézanne might in these circumstances be accepted as a spokesman of the young hopefuls of French art.

Zola miscalculated. In a sense he fared even worse than his friend. His articles raised such a storm of protest that his editor was forced to employ a conformist art critic side by side with him; and as this made nonsense of his tirades, Zola stopped the articles abruptly. He also republished them as a pamphlet, *Mon Salon*. The pamphlet is prefaced by a long and grateful dedication to Cézanne. "We used," he wrote, "to live in our own shadow, isolated, unsociable, enjoying our own thoughts. In the midst of the complacent and superficial crowd we felt lost. We sought for an original voice in every poem and painting. We declared that the masters, the geniuses, created every one of them a world of his own. . . . Did you realize that we were revolutionaries without knowing it? I've just been able to say aloud what we've been telling each other for ten years. . . . You have seen the fine welcome given to our dear thoughts. Ah, the poor boys who lived so healthily in the sun in the center of Provence and ·who cling to such folly and bad faith. For—you perhaps did not know this—I am a man of bad faith. . . . I only praise my relatives and friends. I am evil and a fool. I am a scandalmonger. This, my friend, is very sad and fills one with pity. Will it always be the same old story? Will one always have to talk like everyone else or be silent? Do you remember our discussions? The slightest new truth, we used to say, could not be proclaimed without provoking protests and rousing anger. Now I, in turn, am being insulted and reviled. . . . Yet I am glad to present my ideas for the second time. I believe in

them and I know that in a few years everybody will agree
with me."

3 〜

Zola was right; and though he leaves the impression of
one who enjoyed a verbal fight so much as to forget the
origin of it, he had chosen the painting as he was to
chose the literary form of the future. He nowhere says
explicitly how he acquired the knowledge to defend this
painting; this lengthy dedication to Cézanne is the closest
he was ever to come to an explanation. For though a
natural rebel, Zola was no painter and knew little about
painting. What he knew he had learned for the most part
from his friend, and he took over Cézanne's opinions as
his own. Cézanne was at his worst in exposition but he
had an eloquence of his own when moved and in the
right company; again and again with Zola, crudely but
with the emphasis of right instinct, he had discussed
the road that painting must take. He had commented
again and again on the canvases they had examined together, from the old masters in the Louvre to the official
ones in the Salon and the true ones in the Salon de
Refusés. Zola did not forget comment or discussion; all
went sooner or later into his writings, often enough in his
friend's very phrase when shapely enough. Even the appreciation of Manet, the cornerstone of Zola's position
as art critic, had its foundation in Cézanne's first enthusiasm.

Cézanne did not object to this marketing of his painterly eye. He was generous where he loved. He could even
find a sort of second existence in this journalistic presentation of ideas and knowledge so often born in his own

brain. But he could share little of his friend's satisfaction in this last long attack on the Salon and all that the Salon implied. After all, he had actually painted the rejected pictures. Year after year he had been denied a showing. He had in consequence sold nothing and remained nothing, unknown to all but a tiny handful—in itself a clique—in Paris, and an utterly unimportant group of provincials in Aix.

His dissatisfaction burst out a few months after his return to Aix for the summer of this year, 1866. The outbreak was confided not to Zola but to Pissarro—the first outward sign of Cézanne's growing confidence in him —and took a form which initially seems surprising. "Here I am at home," he wrote, "with the nastiest people in the world, the persons of whom my family is composed, sh . . s above all others. Let's drop the subject."

He could drop the subject but he could not drop the thought. The connection with the Salon, not immediately apparent, was fundamental and explains almost entirely why he tried again and again to get his pictures shown in an exhibition for which he had proclaimed the utmost contempt. The main reason goes back, as so many of Cézanne's actions go back, to his father.

Monsieur Cézanne was by this time a puzzled and disappointed man. He had given up, with commendable restraint he thought, all hope of a son who would make the name Cézanne famous in law and highly respected in finance. With simple faith in a child of his blood he accepted the substitution of a successful painter. In France painting was an honorable profession; men made not only money by it but a name, decorations, a place in society; if Paul chose to enter it, his father would not persist in discouragement but give his blessing. But, the blessing given, everything went awry. First, his son made no real or sustained attempt to enter the Beaux-Arts. When questioned, he declared that the Beaux-Arts was outmoded, was a form of artistic death. He denied that a man must go through the Beaux-Arts to become an accepted painter. He said that genius would out. Then his paintings were rejected for the Salon again and again. They were too good, he said, too original; too far ahead of their time. He spoke of a man called Manet; he was great, he had been rejected too.

This kind of conversation did not prosper, since every word had to be dragged out of Paul. When his father asked why he tried to be included in this despised exhibition, he could only reply that this was the painter's one shop window in Paris. And having admitted that the Salon was essential for the moment at least he was forced into a boast that he would oblige the jury to select him by sheer merit.

The first meetings of father and son on Cézanne's return each summer were therefore less cordial than they might have been. The position was made embarrassing for the son because at heart he agreed with so much that his father said. He had no wish to make a martyr of himself in Paris. He wanted fame and the high regard of men, his father's above all. He wanted the Salon to show him and was bitterly chagrined when year after year it did not. He parted company from his father only in this, that he demanded that he should win fame in his own way; he would make no concessions to convention, officialdom, or anything else.

Even in this Monsieur Cézanne, had he been the painter, would have followed his son; he had been original enough in business. But the necessary effort of imagination escaped him—he was not far from seventy by this time—and he could see no further than the only son who by sheer obstinacy or lack of the necessary talent (and there was nothing much to choose between them) was robbing the Cézanne family of fame and another fortune.

The differences between the two men did not, for all Cézanne's bitter words to Pissarro, seriously affect the family life. Or rather, inessentials were allowed to cloud the real issue. Money, for instance. Monsieur Cézanne's allowance to his son was proving insufficient; he refused to increase it on the grounds that he was giving Paul what Zola had said five years earlier was necessary. This was true and awkward, too. Unanswerable, Monsieur Cézanne thought; but his son argued nevertheless. Argued in vain and was obliged to fall back on Zola for loans with an explanatory "for I am even sadder when I haven't a sou." Not perhaps the clearest of explanations but one which Zola, knowing his Paul so far, accepted with a grimace. He did nothing to smooth relations between father and son, having long since taken the stand that Monsieur Cézanne was a philistine who stood in the way of his son's career.

Cézanne only half accepted this view; he was bedeviled as usual by sympathy with his father. Hence the efforts to get into the Salon. Hence his fury, against the Jury and against his father, when he failed. His father judged by results and could be shown none. In five years not a picture had been sold. There seemed no prospect that one ever would be sold for Cézanne knew well enough that although he had made considerable strides technically in those five years he had still not discovered his "sensation"—the discovery which would at once distinguish him from all other men and turn him from an experimenter into a great painter. He did not tell his father this, but his knowledge of it weakened his defense against Monsieur Cézanne's unspoken attitude,

"Self Portrait," 1879

"Portrait du
Père de l'Artiste," 1866

"Mont Ste. Victoire," 1890

"La Dame à l'Eventail," 1880
Artist's wife, Hortense Fiquet

Émile Zola by Manet, 1868

Cézanne in 1861

At Auvers, 1873

"Le Nègre Scipio," 1866–68

(Museo d'Arte, Sao Paulo)

(Musée du Louvre)

"La Maison du Pendu," 1873

(*Musée du Louvre*)

"Moderne Olympia," 1873

(*Musée du Louvre*)

"Les Peupliers," 1879–82

"Nature Morte à la Soupiere," 1885

"L'Estaque," 1883

"Le Garçon au
Gilet Rouge," 1895

(Collection Bührle, Zurich)

(Musée du Louvre)

"Les Joueurs de Cartes," 1892

that he would have done better to have amused himself
with his painting in spare moments. He stood, in short,
as a failure in the family. His father had agreed that he
should be a painter on the understanding, believed by
all, that he would make a name and money by it. And
here he was, five years later, trying to persuade his father
to increase his allowance, trying in face of the fact,
known to all, that he had refused to follow the course
laid down by Monsieur Cézanne. He still persisted in
declaring that he knew best how to become a successful
painter. The sense in the Cézanne home of long-drawn-
out anticipation was becoming painful.

Paul's reaction to all this was the reaction of all stubborn people with a guilty conscience. Useless to protest
that he felt the power to paint; intangibles weighed
little with Monsieur Cézanne even had his son possessed
a tongue sufficiently agile to explain himself. So Paul
became excessively painterly, growing his hair long,
affecting a "revolutionary beard" and dressing himself
in such a way that Guillemet, down again with his wife,
reported laughingly to Zola that "his rig-out causes a
sensation in the Cours," the main street of the town. His
moods changed with startling rapidity. At one moment
he would tell Pissarro in despair, "I keep on trying to work
but colors are difficult to get hold of here and very expensive. Stagnation, stagnation!" The next moment he
would announce to Guillemet that "now and again the
sky of the future appears less black"—this being high
optimism for him.

As noticeable as the change in his appearance was the
change in speech. He deliberately used bad language with
the cold rage of a tender, sensitive being who doubts
himself. The description is Zola's. Despite characteristic
exaggeration it hit off his friend and the reason for his

confusing change of front. Cézanne was reacting inevitably
to stupidity, and like all tongue-tied and fundamentally
gentle men, when he did force himself to face the world
it was in a manner which did him the utmost injustice.
What he imagined the world thought of him he determined to be. He could not, in fact, be such a man but he
could and did talk like him.

So Guillemet was soon telling Zola: "The Aixois still get
on his nerves, asking if they can come to see his work,
then speaking slightingly of it afterward; so he has found
a good means of dealing with them. 'Go to the devil!'
he says, and those without temperament fly horrified."

This picture of a young man deliberately antagonizing
his townsfolk will be familiar to everyone who knows
how easily extreme sensibility can be driven into rudeness. But Cézanne was not simply sensitive to an extraordinary degree; he passes out of the range of common
experience because he was that rarest of creatures, a man
with the rage to create, and that unhappiest of creatures,
a man who did not know in what manner to create. The
tension set up by these opposites played havoc with his
nerves and made him dangerously difficult company.
Stimulating company, as all great artists are even in
embryo, refusing to compromise, original in thought and
expression; but only a handful of men were to have the
wit and the humility to see the signs of greatness in him.

At home feelings toward him were mixed. All waited
for success to appear, his father sardonically, the women
with fond hope. His swarthy unkempt beard and un-
bourgeois clothes—battered black hat, ancient greenish
coat, blue socks starting out of tattered trousers too
short for the long legs, heavy boots perpetually dirty—
made less stir with his people than in the fashionable
Cours Mirabeau. Except for a few mild protests from

his mother, his appearance went without comment. His father showed perceptivenes by accepting wordlessly this baiting of his fellow citizens; he was not without relish for this treatment of the people who had turned a cold shoulder to him. His sense of humor did him honor, for his son seemed to be digging the grave of Cézanne fame in Aix. As for painting, none understood what he was trying to do, critical judgment was absent. But so also was that commonest of family scourges, the ignorant critic. It was a silent household, the father apart, and the silence outlasted even Paul's experiments.

To judge by Paul's remarks to his few friends, he was living in purgatory. In a sense he was, since non-understanding was a kind of agony to such a nature. But he is found nevertheless painting one portrait after another at home: an excellently posed one of his father, one of Marie at the piano playing the *Tannhäuser* overture with her mother knitting nearby, and one of the young Rose reading to her doll. They were cheap, placid, willing models and their persistent good nature outlasted their infuriating incomprehension of what he was about. Again and again he painted them when bad weather kept him indoors. Perhaps the sight of this hard work, this dedicated slogging, Paul sparing neither himself nor his model, mellowed the father's mind. Whatever the cause, before Paul went back to Paris in January of the new year, 1867, his father had listened to Guillemet's pleading; he increased his son's allowance.

"Cézanne is painting in light tones again," Guillemet told Pissarro after looking at his work, "and I am sure you will be pleased." But what was likely to please Pissarro most of all was Cézanne's own remark, which derived straight from days in the grounds of the Jas de Bouffan and in the country between Aix and the

Sainte-Victoire. The remark was a little revolution in itself and a forerunner of fame: "You know, all pictures painted indoors, in the studio, will never be up to things done in the open air. In depicting outdoor scenes the contrasts of figures on the ground are astonishing and the landscape is magnificent. I have seen some superb things and I must make up my mind to do only things in the open air."

CHAPTER SIX

The Nonconformist
1867–1869

NEARLY four years were to pass before Cézanne began to carry out his promise to paint regularly out of doors—and when he did so, he was driven to it by war.

But this was in the summer of 1870, a far cry from the Paris of 1867, the Paris of the World's Fair, the Paris to which Cézanne returned with hope but anxiety too. He had lost his first dislike of the city and although he was never to feel at home there he welcomed the sense of purpose so lacking in the dreamy heat of Aix. He was ambitious in the highest meaning of the word, he felt that he had something to give the world, he was possessed by the urge to create, which is perhaps stronger in the painter than in any other. In him, certainly, it burned like a fire, was in his eyes, his dislike of the trivial, in the intensity of every word he spoke.

Partly for this reason he remained, as few painters remain, a stranger in Paris. A man possessed makes awkward company and for none more than the painters of that day. Not that they were nonserious; on the contrary the young painters of these years were eager, hopeful, searching to a degree rarely seen before. But fun

was an essential part of their lives; they worked hard,
played hard, too, and in this Cézanne could not match
them; he was altogether too earnest. He was respected,
feared at times, but not loved. To his few acquaintances
he was, according to one of them, "frightening, hallu-
cinatory, like some kind of god in torment. He shut
himself up for weeks at a time. He was always changing his models. He was in despair because nothing he
did satisfied him." He had Zola, but a busy, well-known,
sociable Zola—a Zola far from convinced that his friend
had found his feet in painting. He had the liking and
respect of Guillemet, Guillaumin, Pissarro, Solari, and one
or two others. For the rest he was regarded as a strange,
difficult man and a painter whose struggles to put himself on canvas marked his work with too much effort.
There was, too, a crudity mixed with the force which
offended the tendency of the day. Realism—or, as it had
recently been rechristened, naturalism—was in the air;
the favourite catchword in the advanced painters' cafés
was that beauty was to be found in the most ordinary men
and activities of men. To these young men, a painter who
had to go back in history to discover romance and beauty
was a traitor to his own times and a coward. But Cézanne
seemed to them, as far as they knew his work, to go to
the other extreme; instead of calling a spade a spade and
revealing its hidden beauty he turned it into a threatening weapon. He was not understood and he failed to
make himself understood.

Even more repellent to his contemporaries were his
imaginative compositions. In subject they followed Delacroix—*The Temptation of St Anthony, The Judgment of
Paris* were two of his large canvases—but in treatment
and mood they were all his own and are better ex-
emplified in *The Orgy, The Rape,* or *L'Enlèvement.* The

violence of subject is here matched by harsh treatment
and wild though undeniably effective use of color. But
this form of romanticism—so notably opposed to his still
lives and water colors—was not only outmoded but un-
comfortably close to mere eroticism. The painter, it was
ony too clear, was preoccupied by sex.

Cézanne, ostrich-like, imagining that he could paint—
and remain anonymous—what he dared neither say nor
even consciously think, exposed one of the stumbling
blocks to progress, one of the reasons why he could not
discover his "sensation." For he knew nothing of women.
When he went up to Paris in January, 1867, he was just
twenty-eight, yet in sexual experience he remained like
a schoolboy. But he was not a schoolboy, he was a strong
and passionate man. A frustrated man too, frustrated by
the obsession which had gone far to blight all his youthful years, the obsession that he was unfit or unable to
get on terms with civilized society. He still thought himself hideous to look at, he still imagined that women
shrank from him. This obsession did in fact make him
a little more frightening, since he actually gave himself
something of the illusory repulsiveness simply by imagining it.

The real hindrance was lack of courage, as he was to
prove. But that time was not yet. To console himself
he invented a personality, the personality of the man
who wanted nothing to do with women. This attitude
—as false to him as his oaths and rough talk—he expressed with an "I don't need women. They would interfere with me too much. I don't see what use they
are."

This to a Zola who was making up, in the romance of
success, for what he may have lost by an increasing
plumpness of person. His friend, hot-blooded, romantic,

ardent, idealistic beneath his mask of Provençal ogre, continued to dream of the women he declared he did not want. Imagination, forced to substitute for action over so many years, rebelled, turned sour.

Erotic paintings are not common among young painters; they have more obvious ways of working off natural emotions. Cézanne's violent exhibitionism—himself all unconscious of it—therefore confused the critical sense of his companions. And another manifestation of the same weakness in the painter went far to ruin promising work as well as arouse resentment. "Paul is a dreadful painter as far as the poses he gives figures in the midst of his riots of color," Valabrègue had written not long before to Zola. "Whenever he paints one of his friends it looks as if he were revenging himself for some secret injury."

A perceptive remark; but again Cézanne was innocent of deliberately using his art to express an emotion unworthy of it; he would have been horrified by the suggestion, he the most austere in aim and self-dedication of any man then painting.

Nor was his submission to outside influences always happy. When he showed a penchant for the palette knife after Courbet, he too often used it like a butcher. It was in any case going out of fashion with his contemporaries and his use of it invited criticism. Only when he turned to still lives did he seem suddenly to acquire inner discipline whether he used the knife or the brush. These paintings have a serenity, a rich texture, warm color, and a sense of composition not found at this time in any other work in oils. They had, besides, a pointer to the great painter missed by all, a solidity of forms, a reality and a life rarely found elsewhere; the fruit is eatable, the jugs rest firmly on the table, the clock ticks, the ruck in the cloth irresistibly invites a smoothing hand.

The reason for this ease of handling was not far to seek. In his still lives Cézanne divorced himself for the time from human beings, the cause of all his discontent and self-questioning. Calm came to him. When he painted he was no more the unsatisfied man but painter through and through. More than this, he was the boy who had observed without knowing that he observed the structure of the rocks of the Sainte-Victoire, which had fixed in his mind a sense of natural form and the inevitability of the solidity of the earth's surface, of the continuity of things. His still lives, have, too—and this is cardinal—a feeling of the presence of the unexpressed; the fruit is grown on trees which have their roots in the earth which is poised on the rocks, the jugs have been made from clay dug from the earth; all is part of the unseen core of being.

Here was the great Cézanne in embryo, but none saw it, not even he. His still lives were praised but the still life was not highly regarded by the innovators, it was too common, too obvious, afforded, they thought, too little opportunity of demonstrating the new painting. And the only other form in which he showed distinctive talent—the water colors which he began to paint in 1868—passed with no more mention than the praise of one or two Aix companions whose opinion counted for nothing in Paris. These water colors, in which he rarely used anything but a medley of blues and greens, showed an economy not far from masterly; at times half the surface of the paper was left untouched by the brush. But the water color was even less regarded than the still life. The atmosphere in France did not commonly suit the medium as in England; it had never been and was not then taken seriously by the Paris painters.

Cézanne, then, was judged in these years of the World's

Fair and after on the work which least represented what
he would afterward be, work marred as much by his
personal life and nature as by faults in technique. Two
people were to rescue him, the one from the first, the
other from the second. But their moment had not yet
arrived.

2 ~~~~~

Each year, 1867, 1868, 1869, as in the previous four
years, he submitted his work to the Salon. Each year he
was rejected. Of the young painters, promising or advanced, among the moderns of Paris, all but he had work
chosen in one or more of these years. He alone remained,
after seven years, resolutely ignored. Every day, every
week in winter he met his fellow painters, in the studios,
at Zola's, at Manet's gatherings. Nothing was said but
everything known. He felt more than ever the outsider
and more than ever acted the part. He could write of the
Salon jury, "Well! they will be forever damned in
eternity"; he could believe it, too; but that could not
assuage his fury at meeting men whom he believed in
his heart inferior to himself; it could not assuage his fury
at the thought of the summer descent on Aix, his father's
questions and quizzical glance as he tried to explain
roughly, and how inadequately, why he had once again
been publicly denied as a painter.

In Aix his summers were compounds of long walks to
the Sainte-Victoire and the Barrage, day after day of
painting at the Jas de Bouffan and hour after hour of
absolute despair. He could not hide his feelings from
his few companions. "Paul is an absolute sphinx," said
Marius Roux, a local literary critic, to Zola. "I saw him
at home and we talked a long time. A few days ago we

went together into the country, spent a night there and had lots of time to talk. But all I can tell you is that his health is good. I have not forgotten our conversations. . . . I simply am not sufficiently intimate with Paul to understand exactly what his remarks mean. . . . I believe that he has kept his holy enthusiasm for painting . . . but is subdued by this existence and by his devoted respect for the paternal vermicelli." Fortuné Marion, a geologist and amateur painter, complained to one of his friends of the lack of money which dogged so many of them. But, he goes on, "there are some sufferers among us just as wretched although they have fewer of these troubles—Cézanne, for instance, who has a secure income yet falls into black despairs of morale and temperament." Guillemet told Zola how sad the thought of Cézanne made him feel. "The poor fellow," he wrote, "must suffer like a damned soul after all the attempts to paint into which he throws himself headlong and which, alas, so rarely come off."

No consolation in Aix, then, except for the passing moment which none could take from him when his brush moved under his hand like an angel and his vision took shape on the canvas. Yet, self-critical as well as obstinate, these moments were followed by hideous anticlimax. What he had thought good was no more than moderate. His vision had escaped him at the last moment. He had not reached his impossibly high standard of perfection. The secret, his own secret as painter, eluded him still and the search had to be taken up again. Know thyself: that, he knew, was the first concomitant of success in art. Did he know himself? Could he admit to what he was, drive out the destroyer, leave only the pure creator? Alone, tongue-tied, forever acting a part in public, he could not even express himself in painting. Something was hindering him: what was it? Whichever way he turned frustration held out a befogging hand. He was utterly wretched.

In Paris he was less wretched only because left less to himself. Whatever he might think of his companions and they of him, one thing they had in common, a love of painting, the urge to create and a belief in the future of their art. What this future should be was less clear and led to most of debates at the Café Guerbois, where Manet then held his audiences. He had moved from the Café de Bade as being too popular to this tiny café in what was to become Avenue de Clichy. Every Thursday evening he was to be found there and most other evenings as well, the center of a lively but extremely varied group of painters and critics. This group soon came to be known as the Batignolles group and was treated by hostile official critics as a single manifestation of heretical tendencies. In actual fact the men who argued around the small marble-topped tables in an atmosphere thick with tobacco smoke were agreed on one point only, an abhorrence of academic painting.

Manet, conscious of high talent and not unaffected by the adulation poured on him by Zola, Duranty, and Astruc, inclined by disposition and the tendency of the age toward realistic painting, but was more concerned to score debating points than to advance a positive theory. He affected to despise theories and with some honesty. He found himself hailed by accident of time and talent as the leader of a group of moderns; actually he remained an individual painter, his true ambition being social success; he intended to use his skill to that end.

In a sense Manet could be seen to be an anachronism. He appeared evening after evening at this humble café dressed with extreme care, gloved, caned, and top-hatted, and sparkled with bons mots. Had his authoritarianism not been tempered by a rather vulgar good nature, his reputation as painter would scarcely have saved him from trouble. As it was he met his match in Duranty, an admirable debater, and was in general outclassed by Degas, who with the natural taste of the aristocrat did not appear out of place in any gathering and whose sharp and stinging retorts were difficult to parry.

Zola, the official champion of Manet and advanced painting, played a prominent part in these debates; if he had little original to say on the subject of painting, he said it most effectively and with a pungency and enthusiasm hard to resist. Essentially down to earth by nature despite his early flourish of romanticism, he was proving himself a first-rate journalist of the tough type. His private ambition was to write realistic novels dealing with men and women of his time and class and abolishing all artificial conventions of taste. To him, any fact which illustrated character must be written down; he accepted no limits. This bold conception was held by the painters, too. It was generally agreed in the Café Guerbois that the backward search for beauty was outmoded; beauty was in the eye of the beholder. But the painters did not discuss naturalism with the mind of Zola; they might use the same words, but the thought was different. The whole bent of the writer's mind inclined toward the salacious; Zola was that case, not rare, of the man who makes use of a worthy theory to support an unworthy inclination and is genuine on both counts; to portray a woman going to the lavatory was with him both duty and pleasure.

The painters at the Guerbois were of quite another kind, Manet and Guillemet perhaps excepted; for them the theory and its application was all. They were then more interested in talking than doing, a weakness particularly found in the Paris cafés. The time was to come when Manet would stride in after a railway journey with a "What charming chaps, those engine drivers! I must paint them!" The time was to come when Degas would paint the dancers at the Opera with a brush which stripped false glamour at a glance. But this was not yet; Manet and Degas were still making portraits of their wealthy friends; excellent work, which put the official artists to shame, but adding little to the development of painting.

The discrepancy was not lost on Cézanne. When he looked in at the café he made a point of his disinterest in the debators. Painting, he believed, was no matter of words, nor would he pander to what so often degenerated into a debating match between Manet, Degas, Duranty, and Zola. He felt at a loss when conversation sparkled. He listened ironically. He could not understand the fuss about the common man; such a thing, he thought contemptuously, could only happen in Paris. A typical Parisian novelty, the common man as model! To him who had used him as model in Aix all his painting life, thinking nothing of it, the novelty was not so apparent. What he saw as hypocrisy revolted him. He would not talk of the common man and paint society women!

Nor was he in accord when in the midst of one of his creative moods—not the mood truly reflecting the artist but in which the visionary was led astray by sexual frustration. At such times the discussions at the Guerbois seemed futile and superficial. And more and more, whatever mood he might be in, he saw Manet as a nonserious man, superb technique notwithstanding. How much envy entered into this judgment cannot be said, but essentially, Cézanne, suspicious though he was of a polish he did not possess, expressed his peasant heritage; to him painting was a battle, a long unending fight to wrest from the coarse ground that was himself flowers of spiritual truth and beauty.

He much preferred the quieter members of the Batignolles group and with exaggerated brutality made his preference clear. He would walk into the Guerbois, ancient top coat swirling around the tall, thin figure. The dingy black hat did not cover the froth of black hair around ears and neck. He would stand, stooping slightly, head bent, regarding the company suspiciously from the small fiery black eyes. Then he would shake hands, French custom. But not with all. When he came to Manet, seated as usual at the center table, he went deliberately through all the motions of respectfully re-adjusting his weird dress. He unbuttoned the faded blue jacket and the white linen waistcoat streaked and spotted with paint, hitched up the too short trousers, untied and retied the soiled sash of violent red which supported them. Only then, a perfect foil to the dandified Manet, would he ceremoniously lift his battered old black hat and, exaggerating his Provençal accent to the point of caricature, say nasally, "I won't offer you my hand, Monsieur Manet. I haven't washed for a week."

That insult accomplished, he retired to the back of the room, where he found Pissarro and Monet. With these two he felt more at home. They were the landscapists of the group and the solid men. And although he had not carried out his promise to himself to turn to *plein air* painting, he sensed its rightness for him sufficiently to agree with Pissarro and Monet when they argued with Manet and Degas, who preferred to work in the studio. And he was vitally interested by what they had to say about colors. Pissarro, for instance, claimed that gray is

at the back of all color to be found in nature. To
Cézanne, living in the Midi, where the bright sunlight,
unimpeded by cloud, takes the color out of everything,
the truth of this ought to have been self-evident. It was not
so; seduced by his love of violent color he had accepted
the bright surface. He thought about it, carefully, slowly.
He looked again. And at last: "You are absolutely right,"
he was to write to Pissarro, "to talk so much about gray.
This alone rules in nature, but it is dreadfully hard to
reproduce." At the Guerbois, Pissarro also explained how
this gray could only be built up on the palette as in nature
by the use of color. Cézanne listened and remembered.

Pissarro and Monet talked much and argued much
about the color of shadow. To Manet as to most painters
shadow was black and formed a bounding line which
helped toward the simplification he sought in his painting. They replied that repeated experiments had convinced them that, on the contrary, there were no bounding lines in nature and that the shadow, far from being
black, was just as rich in color as anything out of shadow;
the difference was merely one of degree; the colors in
shadow were simply less bright.

This, too, Cézanne remembered to his profit. But to the
excited talk about oriental art—introduced by the coming
to Paris of Japanese prints and fans and by the World's
Fair exhibits—he lent a deaf ear. This indeed was a cue
for one of the many spectacular exits he would make,
getting up without a word and stalking out. But he
listened with sympathy to the many plans for selling
pictures. Several of the painters there were in the last
stages of destitution. Monet and his Camille had more
than once nearly starved to death, Renoir lived on the edge
of starvation, Pissarro and Guillaumin, who had left his
job to paint, only kept body and soul together by painting

blinds for shop windows. Only Manet and Courbet, neither of whom needed the money, had found an answer to the stranglehold of the Salon; each had had a pavilion built at the World's Fair in which to stage a private exhibition.

This stimulated the unmonied members of the group to plan a group exhibition. There was much excited talk about it, Cézanne wishful to help. But his allowance, even the enhanced one, would not run to a large subscription. Cézanne was generous where the object seemed to him worthy—he had already helped out Solari—but to put such an exhibition on its feet was far beyond him. Beyond all the rest of the young men, too; the exhibition, which would in effect have been the first Impressionist show, was not destined to be held until 1874.

Of all the painters at the Guerbois, Pissarro alone managed to increase his standing with Cézanne. That this was possible revealed not only much of Pissarro but the true nobility of Cézanne. For Pissarro, though a lovable man, was not always an easy one. The oldest of all the painters, nine years the senior of Cézanne, this socialist, atheist Jew from the West Indies held strong opinions which he did not hesitate, which indeed he felt obliged to express. And express cholerically. By rights Cézanne, intolerant himself, should have found him intolerable. But he did not. With an insight which none there would have credited him with, he respected even in the full flow of a Pissarro outburst the essential goodness and single-mindedness of the man. He even listened. He did not always answer back. He knew, as all present knew, the struggle which Pissarro had to live and paint. But he did not know, as was usually the case, through Pissarro's own complaints; the elder man accepted his

sufferings without comment. His art was much greater
than himself—that was always Pissarro's attitude, spoken
or not. And when he fell back into his customary gentle-
ness of manner, great eyes beaming above a patriarchal
beard like a latter-day prophet, Cézanne felt for him
the stirrings of an affection hitherto given only to Zola
and his father. In that Italianate force of fist, as alien to
the pleasant smoothness of the French painter as to
Pissarro's own work, Pissarro alone had perceived at once
the struggles of an artist who might be great, who would
certainly become important. He had said so. He had
maintained his belief against incredulous laughter. He
had offered to help. Cézanne was deeply grateful. In as
far as he could make himself the disciple of any man,
Pissarro was that man.

Zola excepted, Cézanne fell foul of almost all the rest at
one time or another. He could not forever keep silent.
When he spoke it was with some ironically phrased comment at complete variance with all that had so far been
said. But there was no argument. His statement—theories
he despised—questioned, he shut his mouth tight and,
eyes sparkling, left the café without a word. No fare-
wells. No looking to right or left. Nothing.

Cézanne gone, there would be laughs and shruggings
of shoulders. Mad, quite mad. Yet a perceptive listener
would gather that behind the laughs and shrugs lurked
a certain uneasiness, the unease of incomprehension.
That Cézanne was an extraordinarily difficult man was
clear to all. Not so clear, but suspected, was that he
was also an extraordinary man. Even his work, so faulty,
so violent, could not be dismissed. It was not nothing.
It was not nonsense. With all except Pissarro, Guillaumin
and, to a lesser extent, Zola, he forfeited all sympathy.
Nevertheless he worried them.

3

Zola, well in with the leaders, did not care for his friend's tantrums; they reminded him of the boyish outbursts during the excursions about Aix. But Cézanne was no longer a boy, he was a man going on thirty. Would he never grow up? Zola wondered, making Cézanne's excuses as best he could.

This was not the only question Zola was asking himself about Paul. Would he ever find himself as painter—this was even more cardinal if not in truth one and the same question. As the prominent art critic into which he had blossomed, Zola found himself in an embarrassing position vis-à-vis his friend. He could not guess that his limitations and not the limitations of Cézanne were the chief stumbling-block; he did see, however, that his friend had far to go even though he was incapable of appreciating the result when he got there.

His doubts were strengthened early in 1867 when, down in the south, Marius managed to arrange the showing of a single Cézanne picture in a Marseilles shop window. No one was stronger against the existing jury system for the Salon than Zola, but after Marseilles he could scarcely challenge the fact that, as far as Cézanne was concerned, they spoke for the general public. For the picture nearly led to a riot. Valabrègue, reporting to Zola, explained: "People gathered in the street. A crowd formed. It seemed stupefied." There was one dubious gain; many voices demanded to know who had painted the monstrosity and, as Valabrègue loyally put it, "there was a slight *succès de curiosité*." But for the rest, "I think that if the painting had been displayed much longer they would have ended by smashing the window and destroying the canvas."

Cézanne's rage, despair and humiliation—for of course the occurrence could not be kept from his father—can be imagined. Zola, less emotionally involved, nevertheless had his difficulties, the struggle between art critic and boyhood friendship. For a moment the struggle was resolved in Paul's favor. In the Spring of 1867 Zola read in *Le Figaro* (he had himself moved to *La Tribune*) a critical article on the offerings to that year's Salon, embodying extracts from a similar article from another paper. In the article was this quoted passage: "I have heard of two rejected paintings done by M. Sésame (no relation to the Arabian Nights) the man who in 1863 aroused general mirth in the Salon des Refusés—as usual!—by a canvas showing two pig's feet in the shape of a cross. This time M. Sésame has submitted two compositions which, though less queer, are nonetheless worthy of exclusion from the Salon. These compositions are entitled 'The Wine Toddy.' One of them depicts a nude man to whom has just been brought a toddy of wine by a rather overdressed woman. The other shows a nude woman and a man dressed as a lazzarone; in this one the toddy has been spilled."

The fact that the writer had mistaken another exhibit at the Salon des Refusés for Cézanne's did not irritate Zola so much as the deliberate intention to wound. In a fury he wrote to the art critic of *Le Figaro*, having overlooked the original article: "Please be kind enough to insert these few lines of correction. They concern one of my childhood friends, a young painter for whose strong and individual talent I have great respect. You reprinted a cutting from *L'Europe* referring to a M. Sésame, who was said to have exhibited at the Salon des Refusés in 1863 "two pig's feet in the shape of a cross" and who this year had another canvas rejected, 'the Wine Toddy.'

"I am bound to say that I had some difficulty in recognizing under the mask thrust on his face one of my old school friends, M. Paul Cézanne, whose artistic inclinations do not run to the slightest suggestion of pig's feet. Not so far, at least. I make this reservation because I can't see why one shouldn't paint pig's feet just as well as one paints melons or carrots.

"M. Paul Cézanne, in excellent and numerous company, has it is true had two canvases rejected this year: 'The Wine Toddy' and 'Intoxication.' M. Arnold Mortier is pleased to be amused by these pictures and has described them in a manner which does great credit to his powers of imagination. This is all just a pleasantry which one shouldn't think twice about. I am well aware of that. Yet I have never been able to appreciate the kind of criticism which consists in condemning what one has never seen. So may I just be allowed to comment that M. Arnold Mortier's descriptions are inaccurate.

"Even you, my dear colleague, add your opinion: you are 'convinced that the artist may have put a philosophical idea into his paintings.' This conviction is mistaken. If you want to find philosophical artists, look for them among the Germans or our pretty French dreamers. The painters of the analytical school, the young men whose cause I have the honor to defend, are satisfied only with the great realities of nature.

"It is up to M. de Nieuwerkerke to exhibit 'The Wine Toddy' and 'Intoxication.' As you know, a number of painters have just signed a petition demanding the re-opening of the Salon des Refusés. One day M. Arnold Mortier may see the canvases he has described and judged so glibly. Meanwhile it is a fact that M. Paul Cézanne will never call himself M. Sésame and that he

can never be the creator of 'two pig's feet in the shape
of a cross.'

This letter, most typical of the writer at that time, did
credit to Zola's feelings for Cézanne; there is no sign that
he thought well of his friend's offerings to the Salon.
Quite the contrary; for as time went by, his old enthusiasm waned perceptibly. The name of Cézanne remained significantly absent from his critical articles. And
the next year he put into writing, and into circulation,
an opinion which went far to cripple his friend's progress
in public esteem for a long time. He did so in good faith,
no doubt; Paul was an embarrassing man to champion
in any sense; but the result was unfortunate.

The occasion came about when Zola received a letter
from a colleague on *La Tribune*, a man called Théodore
Duret. Duret was to play a considerable part in the
transference of the Impressionist group from a collection
of disparate painters into a group known by all. He was
immensely enthusiastic about modern painting and anxious to help modern painters.

"I've heard of a painter named Cézanne or something
of that kind," Duret wrote, "who comes from Aix and
whose work has been rejected by the Jury. I seem to
remember you once telling me about a very eccentric
painter from Aix. Is that the same as the one rejected
this year? If so would you please give me his address
with a note of introduction so that I can get to know
the painter and his work."

Zola refused. "I can't give you the address of the
painter you mention. He is going through a period of
searching and shuts himself away a great deal. I think
he is quite right not to allow anyone in his studio. Wait
until he has found himself."

Zola's bang of the door has been the subject of much

speculation. Was he envious of something he could not understand, jealous of another influence on Paul, ashamed or apprehensive of the reception Duret might meet? Did he fear that his friend would confound his reputation as critic or would make him a laughing stock, or was he genuinely certain that Cézanne needed time and solitude? All these suggestions and more have been canvassed. The fact that he had told Duret of the "very eccentric painter" suggests that his loyalty to Paul had at times been strained too hard for him. It suggests, too, which was the fact, that the literary man in him was proving stronger than the friend; Cézanne provided magnificent copy for a novelist and Zola was only too well aware of it. And not Zola alone; for Duranty was also making notes on this strange painter with a view to a novel.

Yet in this instance Zola's good faith must be accepted; certainly, his statement was correct—Paul had not found himself. But Paul should have been allowed to say that for himself or demonstrate it in his own way. He was not given this excellent opportunity and to that extent Zola's refusal was unfortunate. A man who is trying to find himself will probably do so most effectively on his own, but knowledgeable encouragement can speed the process. And that Zola now denied him.

The check could have proved serious to a painter who could not obtain a hearing and whose continued allowance from his father might depend on precisely the kind of help that a man like Duret could give. That the check was not more serious was due to a happening with which Zola had nothing to do, the most important event in Cézanne's adult life to that time. This was his meeting with Hortense Fiquet.

Chapter Seven

Hortense

1869–1871

H E met her in Paris in 1869. She was nineteen years
old. She had been born in the Jura, came to Paris
with her mother and father, a bank clerk, and
remained there when he was posted elsewhere. After
her mother's early death, not long before she met Cézanne, she became a model, a common way for girls with
good figures and little education to earn a living. Like
so many Frenchwomen she was sallow-skinned, dark-
haired, dark-eyed. Unlike most Frenchwomen she was
tall. Except for occasional moments of relaxation, when
she wore her abundant hair in a bun on her neck, she
followed the normal hair style, parted in the center and
piled on the back of the head. This pleased the painters,
for it gave her an exceptional length of line from the
top of the hair to the chin. She had a long, oval face
and the other classical attribute, the large, heavy-lidded
eyes. She was far from a beauty, however; her long nose
was markedly aquiline and the lower part of her face
was downright plain, with prominent lips thrusting out
her mouth and spoiling the shape of the jaw.

Cézanne at thirty had taken on the appearance by
which he is best known today. His hair had receded

94

rapidly. The center of his head was bald almost to the crown; at the sides the black hair bushed out to cover the greater part of his ears. He wore a thick dark mustache and heavy beard. His black eyebrows had thickened and, it seemed, drawn even closer to the small, piercing eyes. He looked very much more than eleven years older than Hortense.

He remained a virgin. He rarely saw women and when he could not avoid meeting them behaved "like a boy who tried to ignore them, hiding a painful timidity under a crude form of bluster." Zola noted his friend's embarrassment with fond amusement. His defense varied according to his mood when Zola tried to tempt him into sociability. "I don't need them," he would say when for a short time his painting went sufficiently well for him to persuade himself that work could absorb every emotion. In less confident and more honest moments, which occupied most of his time, he admitted that he had "always been afraid even to try to find out what they were good for."

The studio he had been able to set up since his father increased his allowance was chaotic, dirty, dusty to a degree rare even with a painter. It was the room of a man without a woman; no feminine hand had ever been at work there, no feminine voice ever heard. Outside the studio Cézanne was obliged occasionally to meet women friends of his fellow painters, but the studio was sacrosanct; he refused to allow a woman inside it. Even female models were scarcely ever seen there. Nor was this wholly regard for his work. He feared that he might make a fool of himself and expose himself to ridicule by his clumsiness and lack of bright repartee. He even feared that he might take what he longed for and yet dreaded and awake to disillusionment and deeper self-hatred or self-despising. In that sad workroom of Cézanne his whole life and its tragedy was open to the discerning eye.

When that eye first looked on it is not known, for Cézanne's secretive instincts grew almost into a mania after he had met Hortense. It is not even certain where he met her. The most likely explanation is that he was introduced by Guillaumin, who had employed her as model and who remained one of the very few painters accepted by Cézanne without a horde of reservations: good-natured, generous, unassuming, this happy-go-lucky young man could not tread on the toes of any, not even Paul's.

The date of the meeting can be put with fair certainty toward the end of the year. How Cézanne plucked up courage to speak to her politely let alone to make love remains a mystery; a mystery which sexual attraction and sexual starvation combined can only explain in part. Even then, with Hortense met, a lonely, motherless Hortense who had begun to show her feelings for this difficult man, a definite spur was needed to drive him into action.

This spur was the approaching marriage of Zola. Zola's fiancée was far from hostile to Paul—he is, indeed, rumored to have introduced her to his friend. But his imagination at once built a gulf between himself and an engaged and soon to be married Zola; he would be in the way, would be secretly wished away. And his pride made him act promptly, to withdraw himself from the close friendship before the friend wanted to withdraw.

There was some truth in this as there always is in such cases, but Cézanne exaggerated absurdly the probable loss of intimacy. Being what he was, he sought consolation, and the thought of the virtual loss of Zola gave him courage to grasp it.

Hortense remains to this day a shadowy figure, obscured by the caution of Cézanne. One thing is clear; she had unusual powers of perception. Cézanne went out of his way to obstruct a clear and favorable view of himself. All the worst side was put forward. One thing he could not hide from a woman, his attraction to her. Hortense, divining this, divined much else, for an admired woman is a woman with new eyes. Cézanne's surface faults fell away beneath her clear sight and the true man stood revealed, sensitive, kind, honest, good. And when, early in 1870, he moved to Rue Notre-Dame-des-Champs, she went with him.

2 ⟋⟍

Hortense had come too late into his life to effect any violent change in his nature; that had been fixed in childhood. He did show signs of a new cheerfulness, which persisted through Zola's wedding in May, and dismissed his latest Salon rejection with "I have, of course, been rejected as in the past, but feel none the worse for it. Unnecessary to tell you that I'm still forever painting and that for the moment I'm as fit as a fiddle." This comparative lightheartedness was to peep out often in the next years, but the outward shell of the man—retiring, shy, brusque—remained, as did the caution, rising easily to suspicion, of the child who had failed his father. She could break none of that down; and indeed from what little is known of her, she seems to have had neither the force of personality nor the natural high spirits to affect a strong and melancholy Cézanne to any noticeable degree.

Her role was different but not less important. She gave him confidence and self-respect. Practically, by sitting for him again and again, she saved him model fees and, just

as vital, prevented the outbursts of rage when a paid
model failed to hold the right position—outbursts which
could end in the ripping up of a canvas, and which certainly gave him a bad name among professional models.
Above all she began the liberation of the great painter.
Every painter begins with obstacles, of temperament, of
environment, of sheer lack of skill. Since his first stay in
Paris eight years earlier, Cézanne had gone far to acquire
a technique equal to the demands his genius would make
on it. From this largely mechanical point of view Paris
had done what it could for him. Before he could find
himself as painter, two essentials remained. First, he
had to discover his true "sensation." That was the task
above all others and, until he succeeded in his search,
every other merit was worthless. But to find himself he
had to be himself—all excrescences must be sloughed.
And this led to the second essential, the restoration of
his balance of mind. Here the intimacy with Hortense
was invaluable.

His work soon marked the change of life. At first, as
would be expected, it showed an increase of the eroticism
which had marred so much of his painting. Then, sexually
satisfied, he dismissed unhealthy visions; with nothing
left to feed on they disappeared, never to return.

3

He had barely settled down with Hortense when another event—this time quite beyond his control—drove
him further toward his destiny as painter. In July France
declared war on Prussia. Within a few weeks it was
evident to all that she would be defeated. In the first
days of September Louis Napoleon was forced to surrender at Sedan. Soon afterward Paris was besieged.

Some time before this the Batignolles group disinte-

grated. Pissarro and Monet went to England, Manet
joined the army as an officer, Renoir was called up,
Zola, rejected because of his eyesight, retired with his
wife to Marseilles.

Cézanne, leaving Hortense in Paris, had gone down to
Aix as usual for the summer. He told his mother and
sisters about Hortense. With his father he kept silent.
The fact that Monsieur Cézanne had led the way with an
affair of this kind did not encourage his son to give him
his confidence; quite the contrary, Paul concluded that
his father would be even harsher because he himself had
provided the example. No great claim could be put forward for Hortense; she had neither good blood nor
wealth; the alliance was far from being what the old man
had dreamed of for his would-be famous son, a son who
would in any event inherit a great fortune.

So, fearing the withdrawal of his allowance, then even
more vital to him, Cézanne said nothing. And when the
Prussians began to advance on Paris he sent for Hortense.
Not, however, to Aix, but to L'Estaque, a small fishing port
some twenty miles to the south, near Marseilles, where
he joined her.

He stayed until March, 1871. In one respect these
months staged a comedy, the comedy of Cézanne and his
father, the comedy of Cézanne and the Aix authorities.
Monsieur Cézanne, then seventy-two, had become more
autocratic with the years. His questions could be parried;
his assumption that he had the right to open every letter
addressed to his houses could only be evaded by stealth.
Thus his son is found making surreptitious journeys to
Aix for, as he had not been able to tell all his corres-
pondents where he was going, he had to be on the *qui
vive* for letters addressed to the Jas de Bouffan or the town
house.

The journeys were surreptitious, not only for fear of

meeting his father—the two men agreed tolerably in public—but because he was wanted by the authorities. After
the proclamation of the Third Republic on September
4 all able-bodied men were called to the National Guard.
Cézanne, supremely uninterested in politics, declined absolutely to abandon painting for war, the more so as his
work had just begun to take on a new strength and conviction.

To add to the comic-opera situation, both Monsieur Cézanne and his son were honored by the republians of Aix
who took control of the town; the father was elected to
the town council with Baille and Valabrègue among
others; Paul, nominated by his father, was made a member
of the art committee. The compliment remained empty;
Monsieur Cézanne, not forgetting the rebuff of past years,
did not attend the council, his son could not attend the
committee even if he wished, since he would have invited arrest.

However, this being the Midi where life is not too
earnest, the search for Cézanne, such as it was, did not
extend further than the Jas de Bouffan where his mother
dealt firmly with the police. No effort was made to widen
the search, and Cézanne lived openly and peacefully at
L'Estaque. The affair was of interest chiefly to the local
gossips who made much of it; neither Cézanne was popular and tongues wagged as they can wag only at cafés
in the sun.

The subject of the gossip, apart from his hurried journeys for letters hidden by his mother, now frankly turned
accomplice, was enjoying domesticity for the first time
in his life. And for the first time in his painting life, confined to the country and a part of the country new to him,
his work began to change. L'Estaque has a special beauty
even along a coastline famed for its scenery: the rock-

bound bay, the sunlit islands out to sea, the terraced red-
roofed houses backed by mountains, the pines rising out
of red earth, the brilliant blue of the water, the ships and
factories of nearby Marseilles with masts and smoke rising into the clear air—all this fascinated the painter and
challenged his passion for color.

The conjunction of sexual satisfaction and enforced
absence from town was decisive. Art, he began to realize
then and later said, can only develop from contact with
nature. And at last, four years after his resolve to concentrate on *plein air* painting, he actually did so. The result
was soon seen. His imagination, released from the necessity of inward brooding, found expression in the portrayal
of land and seascapes. His strong dramatic sense spilled
out in studies violently colored, reds, ochres, and black
predominating. By the side of his mature work the L'Estaque canvases look crude; as they are; but this was inevitable; his sense of color was still ungoverned and his excitement over Hortense had not yet settled into simple
pleasure. Nevertheless, far though he had to go, the true
Cézanne, the Cézanne loved and admired throughout
the civilized world, had at last begun to show himself in
the genre which was to make him famous. The way might
not be easy but the direction was clear; he was never to
falter again.

CHAPTER EIGHT

Plein Air *Painter*

1871–1874

IN March, 1871, Cézanne and Hortense moved to Marseilles in preparation for a return to Paris. This return was delayed. The war was over but Paris was in ferment, and from March to May the Commune reigned there. Not until June did the capital regain calm.

During these weeks of waiting in Marseilles, Cézanne went over to Aix; he had no money of his own, had sold nothing, and was still obliged to ask his father for money. He dared not ask for his allowance to be sent to L'Estaque or Marseilles, fearing that if his father knew his address he might come over and unexpectedly discover Hortense. For old Monsieur Cézanne was not only active but suspicious of the long stay in L'Estaque. In a household as close as the Cézannes no secret could be wholly withheld from any one member; and Paul's secret, though kept punctiliously by the women, was kept to the letter only; the fact that they had a secret to keep was only too clear.

Monsieur Cézanne did not guess the secret but sensed it. He could safely have been told, had his son known, for his true fear was that the boy (as he still thought of the thirty-two-year-old man) would make a foolish marriage.

102

As it was, the continued conspiratorial silence irritated him and he vented his irritation in a display of power. The enthusiastic prophecies of Guillemet several years earlier— prophecies which had gained his friend an increased allowance—recoiled on Paul. The old man forgot nothing. Paul was dependent on him, Paul had not sold a picture, had not been admitted to the Salon, was in short a failure: why should he expect to be kept when he had refused to become a lawyer or banker or to study art as all successful painters had studied it?

The argument was difficult to refute and Paul, awkward of tongue, short of temper, and uneasy in conscience, made poor work of it. Yet this was now the price he had to pay for a monthly subsidy. Perhaps he suspected that his father was playing a cat and mouse game—for there was never any real likelihood that Monsieur Cézanne would cut off his only son—and the knowledge of this did not make for harmony.

At last, in June, he got a firm promise of his allowance if he returned to Paris. All attempts to get the allowance increased had failed, for as Cézanne could not give the true reason for his need of more money, every reason that he did give appeared patently unreal to the shrewd old man. He returned to Paris a worried man, for Hortense was pregnant.

There he joined with Solari, married and with a child and making ends meet in those difficult after-war days by "turning out saints at sixty centimes an hour" in a religious emblem factory—an echo of Renoir, who had been forced to paint designs on china to earn a living. The ménage lasted six months. Then, as Hortense needed quiet, they moved in December to Rue de Jussieu opposite the Halle aux Vins, which Cézanne was to paint, and only a step from the river and islands. And there, on January 4, 1872, their

child was born. He was christened and registered as Paul
Cézanne.

2 ～

The coming of the child complicated Cézanne's life. He
no longer felt able to go to Aix in summer since Hortense
could no longer be left in Paris to keep herself as model.
Yet since L'Estaque he had hungered for the country to
paint in. Finally, that area of Paris was not best suited to
the health of a small child, the streets narrow, houses air-
less and dirty, drainage nonexistent.

The problem was solved by Pissarro. The Café Guerbois gatherings had just been resumed although the venue
was soon to be changed to the nearby Café de la Nouvelle-
Athènes. At the Guerbois Cézanne, swallowing his pride,
asked the advice, not of Zola but of Pissarro. He asked
knowing the answer, for Pissarro had for years been trying
to persuade other painters to join him in *plein air* painting. And sure enough Pissarro not only recommended
Pontoise, where he had a house, but typically offered Cézanne, Hortense and baby a roof until they found a place
of their own.

So to Pontoise the three went. The small town thirty
miles west of Paris was picturesquely wooded and grouped
about the river—a painter's dream. The Pissarro household was less ideal; it seemed to be filled with children,
was chaotically untidy, and was ruled by the shrewish
Madame Pissarro, resentful of her husband's unprofitable
calling and furious with him for teaching her sons to paint
and with the boys for wanting to learn the beggarly trade.
Even Pissarro's bluff good humor and refusal to be discon-
certed could not always clear the air. And Cézanne soon
crossed the river and took a room for the three of them
at an inn, the Hotel du Grand Cerf.

Here, at Pontoise, his solid education as painter began. Pissarro had gathered around him a band of young enthusiasts including a weekend Guillaumin, once again forced into an office to earn his keep. Cézanne, painting almost daily with the master, listened and observed with a humility extraordinary in the man, but true to the artist. No greater proof of Cézanne's devotion to his art can be found than this pupil relationship with Pissarro. But Pissarro's enthusiasm and obvious selflessness carried the day with the difficult Provençal as with the rest of the Pontoise group.

"It is possible that we all sprang from Pissarro," Cézanne was to say; and though two painters could scarcely be more disparate than he and his genial teacher it was correct that in two essentials Pissarro put him firmly on the way to greatness. There was, first, his insistence on the value of *plein air* painting, which enabled the painter to observe the effect of light and air on color. "Paint what you see," he said, "and forget all that was painted before our time." And there was his insistence on the light palette. "Use only the three primary colors, and their immediate derivatives," was his rule. And again: "Form can be obtained by the use of color; linear form is not necessary."

He and Cézanne painted side by side day after day. Cézanne began to abandon dark colors. Pissarro could not persuade him to drop his favorite black, but, this apart, his canvases grew lighter, his use of color more skillful. The coming of winter enabled him to portray the light grays never seen at Aix.

Nature also imposed its own discipline. Before coming to Pontoise, Cézanne, as impetuous as painter as he was cautious as a man, used to dash at a painting with dramatic strokes of the brush as though he could not endure delay; as though, too, he was fearful of a plain statement of what he saw before him. This misleading dread of insipidity, a common failing of the passionate temperament, began to drop away after a few months of careful study of the Oise countryside. No obvious drama there as in the south but, to a man with a painterly eye, a subdued glow of color and tone never found under the sun of the Midi.

Following Pissarro's exhortations, Cézanne discovered this hidden charm. He worked hard. Every day he set off, easel, canvases, brushes, and paints strapped to his back, in his hands the tall black stick to become famous, on his head the soft panama hat under which the now massive beard threw up keen eyes and sharp nose. With an immense effort of will he subdued his impetuosity; absolute truth to nature became his guiding principle. He explained with the humility of the great man: "When I begin I always try to paint sweepingly, to give form with the brush, like Manet. But I can't convey my sensation at once, so I add color and keep adding it as well as I can." And his way of adding color was the way of Pissarro, by the use of small brushstrokes. In consequence his work of these years, *The Heritage at Pontoise,* the *Old Road at Auvers,* the *View of Auvers,* the *Street in Pontoise* and above all *The House of Père Lacroix, Auvers,* has a depth and richness never seen before and which make his earlier paintings seem curiously blatant. This placing of countless little daubs of color on the original broad brush strokes at once demonstrated Pissarro's dicta that there is no such thing as a bounding line in nature and that shadows repeat the color around them. They also gave a rich and completely satisfactory tone to every object—satisfactory because true to the laws of light and color. He had discovered, in fact, thanks to Pissarro and to his own intense observation and determination to take pains, that "in the very act of painting, one draws. Accuracy of tone reveals the light and shape of the object. The more harmonious the tone, the more precise the drawing."

Pissarro and he not only painted and sketched each other, they painted simultaneously similar scenes. At first Cézanne, who practiced abnegation as fierily as all his other moods, tried too hard to follow his teacher and the result was a number of weak and quite uncharacteristic canvases. But before the year was out the master was in some respects being overtaken by the pupil. They had, as painters, little in common except the burning wish to be true to their individual vision. What strikes the onlooker comparing their work of this time is the strength of Cézanne, the delicacy of Pissarro; the effects of the one are broad, of the other petite. Even at this early stage it is scarcely possible to deny that, despite the overwhelmingly greater technical mastery of Pissarro, the individuality and originality come in the main from the younger man.

Pissarro was the first to see this. Unlike almost every other painter he had next to no *amour propre*. He loved painting before he loved himself and if a man painted better than he did he was the first to acclaim him. So as early as September, 1872, he is found writing enthusiastically of Guillaumin: "What courage!" for his sticking to painting in spite of the handicap of wage-earning and prophetically of Cézanne: "Our friend raises our expectations. I have seen—I have it at home—a painting of astonishing strength and liveliness. If as I hope he stays for some time in Auvers where he is going to live, he'll surprise a lot of painters who condemned him too hastily."

3 ~~~

One of the less frequent visitors to the Café Guerbois and later to the Café de la Nouvelle-Athènes was a thin, nervy man with a rather big head. Like several there—Nadar the photographer for example—he was not pri-

marily a painter, but an enthusiast. His name was Gachet
and he was to be immortalized in the next decade by Vincent van Gogh. But by the early 1870's he was already
becoming known for his help to struggling painters; he
knew all of them in what was to become known as the Impressionist tradition, beginning with Corot. He was a
nerve specialist in Paris, but had recently taken a big house
at Auvers-sur-Oise, near Pontoise, for the sake of his ailing wife. He spent half the week there, half in Paris.

Dr. Gachet did not meet Cézanne at the café gatherings, though he must have seen him from time to time
sitting silent at the back of the room. Dr. Gachet was not
silent; he had plenty to say. His particular passion was
etching, but his general technical knowledge of painting was excellent; he could and did discuss all the problems raised at the meetings. He knew Pissarro well, as
everybody did, and was very much attracted to him;
they met from time to time at Auvers and Pontoise as
well as in the café. He also had living close to him at
Auvers the painter Daubigny, the man who alone had
spoken up for the Cézanne portrait submitted to the Salon
in 1866.

Inevitably Dr. Gachet met Cézanne soon after the
painter had moved to Pontoise. He was at once interested,
in the man as well as the painter, reading the one correctly
and admiring the other with reservations.

His help was soon needed. Cézanne's contentment at
Pontoise was marred by two facts, one inescapable, the
other temperamental. His lodgings were costing too much
and he was running into debt; already the grocer at Pontoise had a substantial bill outstanding. He tried to persuade his father to increase his allowance. This Monsieur
Cézanne would not do; as far as he knew, his son was a
single man without encumbrances and had no need of

further money. That was the position he took up; in truth
he suspected something of the facts and chose this way of
punishing a son who would not trust him. All he would say
was that he would discuss the matter when Paul came
home. And when would he come home?—for this was
the first summer that Paul, seduced equally by painting
and by Hortense and the child, had not returned to Aix
from Paris.

No help there. The other hindrance to happiness at Pontoise was less irremediable. Pontoise was a busy little town,
Cézanne remained, despite all his satisfactions, a man who
hated publicity. His dislike of a stranger's touch, even of
the physical nearness of other people, was growing into
something not far from mania. He detested being watched
when he was working, could not bear comment. The children who crowded round him when he worked about the
town, the people who came to have a look and make remarks drove him almost frantic. He showed every sign of
relapsing into the irritable melancholy of his solitary years.

Dr. Gachet, observing Cézanne's increasing nervousness
and bad temper with a professional eye, came to the rescue. He found him a cheap cottage in Auvers, then a quiet
village; he offered him the use of his own studio and etching tools; he suggested that Cézanne pay his bills with
canvases, and persuaded the Pontoise tradesmen to accept
them; and he promised to buy a canvas or two himself to
add to his collection of contemporary painters.

Cézanne accepted gratefully. In autumn 1872 he moved
to Auvers with Hortense and little Paul. One has to pay
for patronage, as he discovered; he was obliged to etch
whether he wanted to or not, and made an etching of the
cheerful Guillaumin; and he had to accept the comments
of Dr. Gachet on his work. Fortunately he took to the doctor and the doctor was on the whole a sensible critic.

They differed chiefly on the amount of work to be given to any one canvas. Cézanne, dourly frantic to obtain every nuance of light and shade, would add touch after touch of color with a small brush, and the doctor, after watching him for a while with increasing motions of impatience, would break out: "Now then, Cézanne, leave that picture alone. It's done. Don't touch it any more." He was not always heeded; but sooner or later Cézanne, murmuring under his breath, would put up his brushes and turn to another canvas.

4 ～～～

Cézanne spent the whole of 1873 in Auvers, painting with a frenzy of self-dedication. He tried his hand at everything. Besides his main effort at oil painting, he made etchings, water colors; he sketched and, encouraged by Guillaumin, produced several pastels. He could not bring himself to leave the place where he seemed so obviously to be finding himself as painter and where Pissarro and Dr. Gachet offered a sympathy and kindness a thousand miles removed from the sort of horrified or shocked pity he was accustomed to. Here he was helped to recover self-respect. He would not be likely to keep that self-respect at home; once again he made what excuses he could to his mother and father for failing to take his usual vacation in Aix.

All this time he was troubled by shortage of money. He had another mouth to feed; little Paul, a charming child, needed clothes, and Hortense with the best will in the world was forced to dispense a few francs on herself. Dr. Gachet had been as good as his word; he had bought one or two Cézanne canvases—the first sales Cézanne had made in thirty-four years—but paid little for them. Not that he was mean; Manet excepted, the Batignolles group of painters did not command more than a pittance for their canvases. Besides, the doctor had others to think of in addition to his wife and two children and the Cézanne family; he tried to help them all by purchases, and not least the worthy Pissarro struggling to keep a growing household.

Fortunately for Cézanne, who would otherwise have been driven back to Aix by sheer poverty, he was introduced by Pissarro to another queer character who lived on the outskirts of Impressionism. This was the man known far and wide to the painters as Pere Tanguy. Tanguy, like Dr. Gachet, was to be immortalized in the future by a Vincent van Gogh portrait, but in the early seventies he had already made a substantial niche for himself in the world of contemporary painting. Before the war he used to travel around the outskirts of Paris selling the excellent colors he had ground; in this way he had come to know Renoir, Monet, and the Barbizon painters working in the forest of Fontainebleau, and Pissarro working west of the city. He was specially friendly with Pissarro, both men being strongly radical.

After the war Tanguy, more idealist than his friend, joined the troops of the Commune, was captured by the Versailles army invading Paris, and condemned to death. His life was saved by Degas, who obtained the intervention of an influential friend. Deported for a period, Tanguy decided on his return to set up shop as color merchant. He found a shop in Rue Clauzel and quickly gathered almost all the advanced young painters as clients, for, poor himself and knowing that poverty was unromantic, he tried to help them. They rarely had money and often enough had gone short of a meal. The tender-hearted Tanguy gave them all canvases and colors on

credit; the hungry ones he invited into his tiny kitchen behind the shop, where with intimidating but meaningless
growls Mme Tanguy fed them. In return he sometimes took
paintings he liked with a promise to sell if possible. He
also allowed his back room to be used as a kind of second-
ary Café Guerbois, where the young painters could thrash
out their differences; with the added advantage that, unlike the Café, they could discuss often enough with a canvas or two in front of them to bear out their argument.

Cézanne took an immediate liking to this red-haired,
red-bearded man who in his invariable jersey looked like
a seaman. Tanguy loved his job, was selfless, and had a
queer but undeniable sense of humor, the kind that Cézanne, who did not laugh often, relished with a grim smile.
Like himself, Tanguy had been denied the gift of easy
speech; his wife, a formidable woman, made up the lack,
and when her husband was absent was apt to chase the
painters for their debts—debts which Tanguy would
hoarsely assure them later and in private were not to be
regarded too seriously; when his ship came home, that
would do.

The two eccentrics had many an all but wordless conversation, and Cézanne came to spend much time in the
back room of the shop in Rue Clauzel, puffing away at his
pipe. Tanguy not only supplied him with colors and canvases on credit—a substantial item to the poor painter
—and took paintings in exchange, he really admired the
paintings. He thus took his place with a distinguished
minority in Paris of whom the only members were Pissarro, Guillaumin, and Dr. Gachet. He never wavered in
his admiration and Cézanne never forgot his support.
Loathing display, he was charmed by his new friend's
simplicity; a peasant himself in essence, he loved the
peasant in Tanguy: no fine clothes or fine speech there,

but a homely and kindly common sense. For many years Tanguy's shop was to remain the only place where a Cézanne was to be found for sale.

But this was to come later; at the moment there were no sales, only the boon of free materials and the heartening arrival of another admirer. But this was enough to project Cézanne, feeling increasingly sure of himself, into a fresh burst of work. His landscapes remained the chief and most characteristic work but, applying the same principles to still lives, the principles taught him by Pissarro, he painted some striking studies of flowers collected by Madame Gachet from her adored garden and placed in delft vases. In these he banished all dull and heavy tones; radiant, the flowers shine out of the canvases with a joyful riot of color which reflects the painter's happy emotion.

But it was with his landscapes that he made the most striking progress—progress which gained him two more admirers, one of them a powerful ally who was to affect his immediate future considerably. Daubigny, who had painted on and around the Oise for years, came down to the river one day to find Cézanne painting on the bank. He looked over his shoulder and was astonished, an astonishment that he not only confessed to Cézanne but at once communicated to a friend. He had long since forgotten his championship of the Valabrègue portrait seven years earlier, he had even forgotten the name of its painter. So: "I've just seen an extraordinary piece of work on the banks of the Oise by a young and unknown man —a certain Cézanne!"

Then came Duret. Despite Zola's rebuff, he had not lost his curiosity about the strange Cèzanne, of whom rumors came to him from time to time. Then he heard that this Cézanne was painting, and painting well, in Auvers and that Daubigny had spoken highly of him. He wrote to

Pissarro, who was said to have some of the later Cézanne canvases at Pontoise: "I should very much like to see some examples of Cézanne's work in your house, for in painting I look more than ever for sheep with five legs."

Pissarro, always anxious to forward the fortune of another painter and with an insight and selflessness denied to Zola, replied at once, "If you're looking for sheep with five legs, Cézanne is the man for you. He has made some very curious studies which have been uniquely observed."

Duret came. He was impressed. This was in the beginning of 1874, a momentous year. For it was then that at last the Batignolles painters put themselves before the public.

CHAPTER NINE

Impressionist

1874

T HE disastrous war of 1870–71 and the fall of Louis Napoleon came to the unknown painters as a breath of hope. France, abandoning dreams of military glory, turned into herself. She became respectable. She also became rich. There was plenty of money in the country; the world had been amazed by the speed with which the enormous German indemnity was paid. Paris was again a prosperous city, the artistic center of the world. And more than ever the Frenchman dedicated himself to the making of money; railways were built everywhere, factories sprang up, shops multiplied, large stores appeared, a wealthy middle class emerged and took over power. Their opportunities for investment outside France temporarily restricted, the *nouveau riche* looked elsewhere. A part of this elsewhere took the form of the purchase of pictures. The long tradition of art in France was handed on to this new class; they became interested in pictures because it was their heritage, because a picture carefully chosen and shrewdly bought represented an investment, perhaps a very profitable one, and because, anxious to raise themselves socially, these arrivists knew that the flaunting of good original paintings in their houses and apart-

ments was one of the best ways to impress aristocratic
and upper-class visitors.

The problem of the nonacademic painter was, how to
persuade these people to buy Monets, Pissarros, Renoirs,
Cézannes as well as the smooth nonsense served up to them
in Salon after Salon. The answer seemed, at first, through
a dealer's gallery. For Monet and Pissarro had met, in
London during the war, Paul Durand-Ruel, a dealer who
interested himself in their work. He had already published
a sumptuous illustrated catalogue of contemporary paintings with an introduction by Armand Silvestre, a critic
often to be seen at the Guerbois. Most of the leading figures at the Café had work reproduced in this catalogue—
Cézanne was conspicuously left out—and Monet and Pissarro canvases at the Durand-Ruel gallery began to sell
at fair prices. There was a general feeling that Durand-
Ruel offered the long-sought alternative to the Salon.

This hope seemed to be vain when the after-war boom
was followed by the customary slump. The slump, though
temporary, lasted long enough to drive Durand-Ruel into
liquidation. The prices of progressive pictures fell cat-
astrophically. Again the Salon seemed to present the one
hope of sales on which a painter could work and live.

Monet and Pissarro, however, had other views. The
fact that their canvases had once fetched good prices
encouraged them to believe that they would repeat their
success if the public could see their work displayed.
Monet decided to try to organize an exhibition among the
old Guerbois group. His first concern was to stop his col-
leagues from trying to exhibit at the Salon. All except
Manet and Renoir agreed to refrain, and Renoir, rejected by the jury, promptly came over to the side of the
majority. Manet, furious at being "left in the lurch," was
not only accepted but won his first great public success.

This, he claimed, proved his point that the Salon was the logical avenue for his fellow painters to follow. To them, however, it proved precisely the reverse, for the canvas which made Manet popular was a retrograde piece of work, *Le Bon Bock*, somewhat like an imitation of Frans Hals, and showed that the Salon selection committee remained hopelessly reactionary.

This was in 1873. After prolonged discussions a group exhibition was arranged for the spring of 1874, to open just before the Salon of that year. Of the Guerbois crowd, Manet, Fantin-Latour, and Guillemet refused to exhibit. They were supported by Duret, who agreed with Manet's view, and by the aging Corot, held in great esteem by many of the Batignolles group, who told Guillemet on hearing of his refusal, "You've done well to escape from that gang!" Guillemet had moved far to the right since the enthusiastic months at Aix; he saw little of Cézanne, believing him to have taken the wrong direction in painting, but he remained well disposed.

The same could not be said of Manet, who gave as one of his reasons for not exhibiting "Get myself mixed up with that buffoon! Not likely!" There was in this contemptuous remark some pique, Manet not forgetting Cézanne's ironic salutations and general air of disdain at the café. But it expressed a great deal of genuine disapproval, too. He disliked everything about Cézanne's work except its color. Nor was he alone; of the six-man committee which arranged the exhibition and issued invitations to other painters to show their work, only Pissarro was in favor of inviting Cézanne. The other five, Renoir, Sisley, Monet, Berthe Morisot, and Degas, all objected in varying degrees both to Guillaumin and to Cézanne. In the case of Guillaumin they were concerned solely with his work; Pissarro, his champion, soon persuaded them to admit him. But Pissarro had to fight much harder to get Cézanne accepted. Unlike the friendly Guillaumin, Cézanne was not personally popular. To Berthe Morisot, a friend and admirer of Manet, he was a boor. To Degas, the caustic-tongued city lover who disliked landscape painting, he seemed slightly touched. To all five his work caused concern; they did not understand it and they feared that it might prejudice visitors against the movement as a whole.

Pissarro, bushy beard waving vigorously, impassionedly defended his protégé, as he had come to think of Cézanne: innovators themselves, how could they shrink from a still greater innovator? Apart from Renoir, a happy-go-lucky young man less interested in the forthcoming exhibition than most, Pissarro convinced no one. Even if Cézanne's personal oddities were put to one side, the way he kept himself to himself, his dark, suspicious looks, his refusal to talk about his work, the work itself remained. In his introduction to the Durand-Ruel catalogue, Silvestre had described the work of the Batignolles group as "above all harmonious . . . its whole secret a very delicate and precise observation of relationships of tone." It was also, he thought, "singularly cheerful . . . a golden light floods their pictures; everything in them is gay, clear, springlike." This, as a rough generalization, was true. How could Cézanne be said to conform to it?

Nevertheless, Pissarro was insistent; indefatigably he argued, defended, praised Cézanne. It was also the fact, as the others well knew, that the exhibition was not to be confined to the Batignolles group. Monet and Pissarro, the originators, had wished it to be so. Degas held out; he insisted on the presence of friendly painters whose work was less revolutionary; this, he claimed, would tend to make the public more sympathetic. Degas, apart from Berthe Morisot, was the only member with money, the only one with an entree to good society. He would bring in the greatest number of exhibitors and so reduce the cost of contribution per member, an important point to the chronically hard up. He carried his point. So, boomed Pissarro, if they admitted painters at one end of the scale, some of them actually Salon exhibitors, why not admit a painter at the other end, the truly revolutionary Cézanne?

Eventually they gave way; not so much because they were convinced—they remained generally hostile to Cézanne's work—as because all loved Pissarro. Cézanne was accepted.

2

The exhibition of *Société anonyme des Artistes peintres, sculpteurs et graveurs etc.*—the only title on which all could agree—opened on April 15 in Nadar's studio at 35 Boulevard des Capucines, which he had just vacated and offered to his friends rent free. It lasted one month and was the Salon des Refusés all over again. It was a complete failure. Many people visited it but only because it quickly became notorious as the city's latest joke; inside the gallery little was to be heard day after day but howls and screams of mirth as groups, doubled up with laughter, moved from picture to picture. Some wag explained with mock seriousness that these modern painters had a simple way of covering their canvases; they simply loaded a pistol with tubes of paint and fired. This explanation went the rounds of Paris.

Such of the critics who deigned to attend the exhibition demolished it in the same spirit. Monet, Renoir, Pissarro, Sisley, Degas were all attacked and their work ridiculed. But this was not the worst of it; the general fear about admitting Cézanne was borne out; the critics re-

served their choicest blasts for him. He had included three
canvases. Two were landscapes of Auvers. The third, *A
Modern Olympia,* was one of the most remarkable works
of the younger Cézanne. First, unexpected to all who think
of him as forever dour, is the humor in this brilliant take-
off, even to the vulgarity, of Manet. Second, the bold and
confident draughtsmanship. Third, the blaze of color su-
perbly applied. Dr. Gachet bought this picture, Pissarro
with wise insight praised it. These were lone voices. It
was almost as though the painter had determined to defy
critic and public alike. The critics took up the challenge,
the public followed; this picture became the butt of the
show.

A long and facetious article in *Charivari* was given the
title of "Exhibition of the Impressionists"—a name which
was to catch on and to be accepted willy-nilly by the
painters. The critic purported to be showing round the
exhibition an academic landscape painter, one Joseph
Vincent. This is a specimen of his wit: "Suddenly, on
catching sight of *La Maison du Pendu* by M. Paul Cézanne, he uttered a loud cry. The stupendous impast-
ing of this little jewel completed the work begun by the
Boulevard des Capucines—Père Vincent became delir-
ious. . . . 'Talk to me of the *Modern Olympia.* There's a
thing really well done.' But just go and look at it! A woman
bent in two from whom a negress is lifting the final veil
so that she can be revealed in all her ugliness to the bewitched stare of a puppet in brown. Do you remember
the *Olympia* of M. Manet? That was a masterpiece of
draughtsmanship, accuracy, and finish compared with
this thing by M. Cézanne. . . . Père Vincent began to
dance a scalp dance before the bewildered commission-
naire, crying in a stifled voice: 'Hurrah! I'm Impressionism on the warpath. I'm the vengeful palette knife, the

Boulevard des Capucines of Monet, the *Maison du Pendu,*
and the *Modern Olympia* of M. Paul Cézanne. Hurrah!
Hurrah!' "

The other critics followed his lead. Cézanne, said a
woman critic commenting on *Modern Olympia*, "strikes
one as being a kind of madman painting in the midst of
delirium tremens." And another well-known critic exclaimed with typical tastelessness after damning the Cézanne canvases: "Of all known or imaginable juries not
one ever considered even in dream the possibility of accepting work by this painter who used to present himself
at the Salon carrying his canvases on his back like Jesus his
cross."

3

Only one man could have put the case for the exhibitors in a way which would have forced the public to
listen. That man was Zola. But Zola remained silent. The
other Guerbois critics, Duranty, Astruc, Silvestre, re-
frained either from cowardice or sympathy with Manet.
Zola had plenty of courage. He, too, felt sympathy for
Manet (the two men were not unlike) and still admired
his work, but this was only one reason for his silence. He
went to the exhibition and wrote a description of the behavior of the crowd, but this description he reserved for
a future novel. That fact explains much of his changed attitude. He was moving away from painting; he had become the realistic novelist, using everything as copy, his
own feeling for painting, his friends' mannerisms. Already
he had published a novel, *Le Ventre de Paris*, in which
one character, a painter, bears the marks of Cézanne. This
was merely a trial for something bigger which he had in
mind, but it was symptomatic of the man. He had become

the slave of his work; all had to go before it, even loyalty, even friendship. And secretly he believed that Cézanne would never develop the genius in himself.

Zola's withdrawal was accepted by his friend with the true humility of a great man. Cézanne was not to love many people in his life but he loved those few well. Tenacity was in his blood. And to love, for him, was to accept. If Zola was too much occupied with his chosen work to see him often, to come to the Guerbois or Nouvelle-Athènes, to defend the exhibitors, Cézanne accepted the fact without question. He might feel sad, but he did not complain; he loved Zola and believed him to be a great writer who must do as his artistic conscience dictated. Had he known to what extent his friend misunderstood his own work he might have rebelled. But he did not know and did not seek to know. He felt himself to be on the right path but that was all; he had far to go and he knew it.

So Zola's withdrawal, which could be seen as a kind of treachery and which certainly threw his old companion to the wolves, passed not only without a quarrel, but without a hard or reproachful word from Cézanne. The savagery of the critics must have wounded him, but he kept his feelings to himself. He showed them only by his actions. Paris with its cleverness, backbiting, malice, and lack of genuine fellowship suddenly became unbearable to him. When the exhibition ended, choked by the words he would not speak, he left for Aix.

CHAPTER TEN

Laughingstock

1874–1877

CÉZANNE had not seen his parents for three years. Never before had he stayed away from Aix so long. They had protested, once certainly, probably more than once against his prolonged absence; they were growing old, perhaps had not long to live; Madame Cézanne was then fifty-nine, her husband seventy-six. Cézanne answered one of these protests with a letter which was inevitably a mixture of truth and untruth. "You ask me in your last letter why I am still not coming back to Aix. I've already explained that I enjoy being with you much more than you seem to think. But once at Aix I'm not free any more. When I want to go back to Paris I always have to struggle to get my way. And though you don't go so far as to forbid me to leave, I'm very much upset by your unspoken resistance to the idea. I beg you earnestly not to hamper with my freedom of action. Then I could hurry back to you with nothing but joyful feelings. I ask Papa to give me 200 francs a month. This would enable me to stay for a long time at Aix and I should take much pleasure in working in the south, which offers me so many opportunities for my painting. I beg Papa to agree to this request. Then I think I shall be able to continue my studies in the Midi."

Cézanne was replying to his father's blackmail with a little blackmail of his own; very tentative, however, and based on the hope that whatever happened his father would not cut him off with nothing. He did not trust Monsieur Cézanne to accept a *fait accompli*, though there is no reason to suppose that he or Hortense would have suffered by candor and there is some reason to believe that they would have benefitted. But Cézanne from a child had always underestimated his power over his father. He saw simply an autocratic man who kept a tight hand on the purse strings. He forgot the lesson of the astonishing laxness during the six years of roaming with Zola and Baille, he forgot the remarkable ease with which he had thrown overboard his father's cherished hopes for himself, he forgot the significant recommendation of himself for a place on Aix's art committee. Had he been less under the spell of his father's strong personality he would have realized that as the only son of a man of peasant tradition he could dictate his own terms; he was the sole hope of the family and if his aims were honorable his father would be bound to support them. But affection, particularly of child for parent, blinds. All he could realize was that his allowance stopped the moment he returned to Aix and that Hortense and the child would be left dependent on what he could get out of his father. Moreover, being under his father's eye, he would have very little excuse for demanding more than he had received during the Aix holidays years earlier. Hence the attempt to secure a fixed sum before he returned.

In the end he went back because of the failure of his hopes, a year or more old, that the exhibition of the co-operative (the name they used for the exhibitors) might result in sales sufficient to lighten his dependence on his father. Whether Monsieur Cézanne agreed in advance to the payment of 200 francs per month at Aix is not known; if he had not, he was soon persuaded to by his son in person, for within a month Cézanne was writing cheerfully to Pissarro. This letter, a revelation of what Cézanne could be, given trust and affection in a friend, breathed high spirits. His anxiety about the little Paul—for Hortense could not write to him for fear of the letters being discovered by his father—was set at rest by Valabrègue, newly come from Paris. His anxiety about his future was also soon stilled: "I'll tell you nearer the time when I'm coming back and how much I've been able to get out of my father." But "he has agreed that I shall return to Paris— and that's already a great deal."

He made a witty comment on the official triumph of Guillemet at the Salon: "which goes to prove thoroughly that by following the path of Virtue one is always rewarded by men if not by painting." And he gave a not less witty report of an interview with his old Aix academy master who, "seduced by curiosity after reading the Paris papers on the co-operative, wanted to see for himself just how far the Peril to Painting had really gone.To my protestations that an examination of my work wouldn't give him a very good idea of the lengths to which the evil had spread, and that for this he ought to see the work of the great criminals in Paris, he replied, 'By looking at your efforts I can very easily make myself conversant with the dangers threatening Painting.' So he came, and when I told him, as an example, that you replaced modeling by the study of tones and tried to make him understand this by reference to nature, he closed his eyes and turned his back. Nevertheless, he declared that he did understand and we parted in good terms with each other. But he is a good chap and urged me to persevere because patience is the mother of genius etc., etc."

The tone of this report demonstrates a change of moment in Cézanne. A few years earlier a catastrophe like the Impressionist exhibition and still more the savage attacks on him would have crushed him to the earth. Now hard words could hurt but not break. He knew that he was on his true road—a knowledge which his summer months at Aix helped to strengthen. All that he did there helped him further toward self-knowledge: the days and weeks of painting at his beloved Jas de Bouffan, the walks to the dam and the Sainte-Victoire, and even more his sketches of the mountain. For at last he was beginning to look at that exposed rocky body with new eyes—eyes cleared by the years with Pissarro and by work which pointed the direction he must take.

This new confidence was expressed clearly in a letter to his mother—one of the few to be preserved—written soon after he had gone back to Paris in the autumn. Madame Cézanne, fearful that her son and the grandson she had never seen might suffer privation, had arranged to send a case of provisions to Rue de Vaugirard, where Cézanne had temporarily taken rooms for Hortense next door to Guillaumin before leaving for Aix. Were all well? she asked. And he, speaking obligatorily in his own person, reassured her: he—that was to say all three—was well.

But he went deliberately beyond her meaning. He was not only well physically; there was something more and something more important. He replied to her command to give the Pissarros affectionate greeting from herself and her husband—for both parents liked the sound of this man who had gone out of his way to help their son—with a "Pissarro has not been in Paris for a month and a half, he is in Brittany, but I know that he has a good opinion of me, who have a very good opinion of myself. I begin to think myself better than all those around me

and you will know that this good opinion I have of myself has only been arrived at after deliberate thought. I
must go on working away, but not to add the finish which
wins the admiration of idiots. . . . I must try to perfect
what I do for the pleasure of reaching greater truth and
knowledge. And believe me, the time will inevitably come
when I shall compel recognition and win admirers much
more ardent and more convinced that those who are only
flattered by sham appearance."

2

This confidence sustained him throughout another year
of work in Paris and in Aix and was stimulated in the
winter of 1875 by a meeting with his second amateur admirer and collector. Victor Chocquet was a customs su-
pervisor who had begun to build up a collection of works
by Delacroix. He was a man of independent judgment and
when, early in the year, the hard-pressed Monet, Renoir,
and Sisley, kindly joined by Berthe Morisot, put up some
of their pictures to auction, he bought several, undeterred
by savage public criticism. He also commissioned Renoir,
whose work he preferred, to make a portrait of his wife.
Having expressed interest in the Impressionists in general,
he was later taken by Renoir to Père Tanguy's shop to
see one or two Cézannes. He was immediately intrigued
by them and bought one on the spot, though he expressed
a humorous fear of his wife's reaction: "How fine this will
look between a Delacroix and a Courbet!" he exclaimed.
His wife won over, he asked to meet Cézanne. Renoir
introduced him, and the two so different men, the suave,
gentle Chocquet, golden-haired and bearded, and the
dark, sultry Cézanne at once found a bond in their common admiration of Delacroix. Cézanne took him to lunch

at Monet's; they were soon seeing much of each other
and Cézanne began the first of many portraits of his new
friend. For his part, Chocquet constituted himself an unofficial defender and interpreter of the Impressionist movement in which he placed Cézanne at the very top.

Chocquet's purchase and his admirations were Cézanne's
only tangible satisfactions that year. He had moved with
Hortense and the child to Quai d'Anjou, where Guillaumin had already found a studio, and the two painters
worked together by the river, happily enough but without
making a sale. Cézanne began to fret, as he had fretted
so often before, at the sense of confinement in Paris; he
longed for the country. He was disturbed, too, by the
friction which rent the Impressionists. There was talk of
a second exhibition the following year, but the true Impressionists were reluctant to show once again side by
side with men who had joined the first exhibition simply
for the sake of friendship and whose work did not conform to the principles worked out by Monet and Pissarro.
The wrangle disgusted both Cézanne and Guillaumin.
They talked the matter over and decided not to exhibit.
Cézanne returned to his old ambition—shelved during the
past year or so—to force a way into the Salon.

Long before the second Impressionist exhibition opened,
in April, 1876, he had gone south, to Aix, then to L'Estaque
with Hortense and Paul. His father, though still hale and
hearty, left the town seldom, and his mother, greatly daring, rented a small apartment at L'Estaque so that she
could see something of her grandson—an excursion which
she was to turn into a habit. It was at Aix and again at
L'Estaque that Cézanne heard through Chocquet of the
fate of the exhibition, a fate almost exactly similar to the
first; laughter by the crowd, abuse by the critics. Some

voices were raised in the painters' favor, including those of Duret, converted wholly to Impressionism, and of Chocquet, who practically lived in the Durand-Ruel gallery where the show was being held. But the net result was as before: ridicule and virtually no sales. Monet alone scored one big success, selling a picture for the large sum of 2000 francs.

Cézanne had been rejected once again at the Salon, a rebuff which he accepted as philosophically as he was able, with "I almost forget to tell you that I've been sent a certain letter of rejection. This is neither new nor surprising."

This was to Pissarro, who, deeply dejected and harassed by lack of money and his wife's understandable nagging, complained of the break in unity—Manet still refusing to exhibit, Monet become very friendly with Manet, all the rest at sixes and sevens.

Cézanne, working desultorily on sea and landscapes, praised the Midi for all the year round painting: ". . . the vegetation doesn't change here. It consists of olive and pine trees which always keep their leaves. The sun is so fierce that it seems to me that the silhouettes of objects are not just black and white but blue, red, brown, and violet. I may be wrong, but this appears to me the antithesis of modeling. How happy our gentle landscapists of Auvers would be here. . . ."

In his contentment he allowed affection for Pissarro to sway his judgment; Monet's friendship with the by now detested Manet, his successful sale, his differences with Pissarro all turned the impetuous southerner against him. There was already talk of a third exhibition, which Pissarro wanted cleared of every non-Impressionist (for whom he now used the word "co-operative" intended sarcastically), and Cézanne, who was thinking of returning to the fold, burst out with "I hope that our co-operative Exhibition will fall flat if we have to show with Monet. You may think me a blackguard, and perhaps I am, but one's own future must come before everything else. . . . On the one hand, too many shows in succession seems a bad idea to me, and on the other, visitors who expect to see Impressionists may find only co-operatives."

Having said this and much more, he excused himself for his pungency: "I put these ideas before you, a little crudely perhaps, but I'm not noted for extreme tact. Don't be annoyed with me; when I come back to Paris we can discuss it; perhaps we can arrange to sit on the fence. If an Impressionist background can help me I shall exhibit the best things I have with them and offer something neutral to the Salon."

This, too, sounding perhaps insufficiently placatory, Cézanne spoke with the honest gruffness that Pissarro at least would not misinterpret: "My dear friend, I shall end by saying with you that as some of us share a common aim, let us hope that necessity will oblige us to act together, and that interest and success will strengthen the bonds that good will has often seemed inadequate to consolidate."

He added a characteristic note. Enraptured he might be by the southern scene, but the southerners were not always enraptured by him; as in Pontoise, he resented onlookers, and in the sleepy little village of L'Estaque men and children alike had all the time in the world for gazing at a painter at work. Nor was his painting approved of any better than his manner. So: "If the eyes of the people here could strike dead, I should have been b . . . . . . d long ago. My face doesn't please them."

3 ~~~~

Cézanne did join the third Impressionist show. Back in Paris in the autumn, he had his promised talks with Pissarro. All was well. The rift between Monet and Pissarro —an artificial one, since both had similar aims—was mended. Even the adverse comments of Duranty, imperfectly veiled, did not move Cézanne. Duranty, who was secretly using Cézanne as the model for an eccentric and unlikeable painter in a novel, wrote in 1876 a booklet on the second exhibition. In this he showed much sympathy with the Impressionist doctrine and theories but expressed many reservations about the group which, he said, included "original personalities side by side with eccentric and ingenuous characters, visionaries side by side with profound observers, naïve ignoramuses side by side with scholars . . . real joy in painting side by side with ill-advised efforts which merely irritate the nerves. . . ."

Cézanne, although he had not exhibited, was clearly indicated, but the admiration of Pissarro, Chocquet, and Dr. Gachet and the stimulation of fresh sales, this time to a stock-broker friend of Pissarro named Gauguin, helped him to brush off this criticism from a supposed ally.

The third Impressionist exhibition owed its existence chiefly to a new admirer. Gustave Caillebotte, a young and wealthy engineer and amateur painter, met Monet at Argenteuil when the painter worked there in the summer of 1874. Taking an instant liking to Monet and to Renoir, whom Monet introduced him to, he began to buy their pictures and to learn their style of painting. He soon extended his admiration to Pissarro and Cézanne, making a point of buying canvases which seemed unlikely to sell elsewhere. By the end of 1876 he had come

to feel so strongly about Impressionism and its main ad-
herents that he made a will leaving his collection to the
Louvre and making generous provision for a first-rate
exhibition. And when, in the early months of 1877, the
proposed third exhibition seemed likely to founder for
want of money, he came forward and discovered and paid
for a suitable show place. "The show will be held," he
assured a troubled Pissarro. "It must be." No regular
gallery being available, he rented the second-floor apartment of a house in Rue le Peletier, near Durand-Ruel's
gallery.

There, in April, the third exhibition opened. Eighteen
painters exhibited as against the thirty of the first exhibition—the lukewarm were being weeded out—and
both Cézanne and Guillaumin showed for the first time
a good selection of pictures.

Cézanne not only brought three water colors and
thirteen canvases, including still lives, landscapes, and a
portrait of Chocquet, but was given the place of honor
—the walls of the main drawing-room—jointly with
Berthe Morisot. The honor—the hanging committee consisted of Pissarro, Renoir, Monet, and Caillebotte—was
not appreciated by any of the visitors except Chocquet
and a young critic friend of Renoir, Georges Rivière.
After a comparatively sober opening, the exhibition was
turned into farce by the press. Not only critics but
cartoonists got to work. Once again there were gales of
laughter, witty remarks and rude ones in front of the
pictures. And in no place was the laughter so asinine as in
the main room, where the crowds gathered to jeer before the wall on which the Cézanne pictures were hung.
For the second time he was made the *enfant terrible* of
the Impressionists.

Nothing could better illustrate Cézanne's position than

the fact that he found himself one evening at the dinner table of Nina de Villard. In the sixties, as Nina de Callias, this wealthy and eccentric young woman had made her house the talk of Paris by her championship of the Parnassian poets and every other artistic underdog she could attract to her soirees. Since then, becoming too much involved in politics, she had lost power. She still held her soirees but her aim had changed; she sought to exhibit the latest notoriety. In that role Cézanne was invited. Some faithful admirers of the sixties hung on. Chief of these were the creole poet Léon Dierx, the raconteur and writer of horror stories L'Isle Adam, and the musician Ernest Cabaner. One of her former stars, Manet, who had made two striking portraits of her, had withdrawn himself when she lost caste, and Cézanne was one of the rare painters to be seen in her salon. Although taken to the dinner by Dierx, and meeting at table an Aixois in Zola's poet and journalist friend Paul Alexis, Cézanne typically attached himself to Cabaner. He knew nothing of music, but he recognized a good man when he saw him. The gentle, dreamy Cabaner, composing an oratorio while he played in a cheap Left Bank café to keep himself alive, was a man after Cézanne's heart; unworldly, both of them, Cabaner was in manner what Cézanne could never bring himself to be, loving and generous. Cézanne liked neither frivolity nor late hours. He did not go to Nina's again. But he did not forget Cabaner.

At the exhibition Rivière was doing his best; he brought out a little paper, *L'Impressioniste,* while the exhibition lasted, explaining why the painters painted as they did and emphasizing their merits. Cézanne he rated particularly highly. "The most attacked painter," he wrote, "and the worst treated by press and public for the last fifteen years, is M. Cézanne. There is no outrageous epithet which has not been fixed to his name. His works have successfully attracted the most ridicule and continue to do so." But, claimed Rivière, although people stood before a Cézanne canvas "so that they can have a good laugh," he knew of no work less laughable. "In his paintings M. Cézanne is a Greek of the great era; his canvases have the calm and heroic serenity of the paintings and terra cottas of antiquity. . . . He is a great painter. . . . His still lives, so precise in their relationship of tones, possesses the solemn quality of truth. In all his work he evokes emotion because he himself experiences a violent emotion in the face of nature and transmits it by his craftsmanship to the canvas."

Inside the gallery Chocquet, who was there day after day from the hour of opening to the last minutes, tried word-of-mouth tactics. He would fearlessly buttonhole a jeering group, "challenged the laughers, made them feel ashamed of their jokes, lashed them with irony." Sometimes he fastened on to a solitary lagger, "dragging him almost by force before the canvases of Renoir, Monet, Cézanne, and trying to make him share his admiration. . . . Persuasive, vehement, domineering by turn, he devoted himself tirelessly."

Thus Rivière, watching this mild man fight for the painting of the future. Duret saw him too. "He became a kind of apostle," he said. "He got nothing but smiles and mockery but was not cast down. . . . I remember seeing him trying to persuade famous critics and hostile artists who had come simply to run down the exhibition. . . . He always had the right word when defending his painter friends. He was specially indefatigable on the subject of Cézanne, whom he placed on the highest level."

All in vain. Chocquet simply aroused amusement for

his "gentle insanity." Rivière was known to be an admirer and his writing was read as propaganda. Neither could halt the inevitable. After the exhibition closed—an absolute failure as to sales—the name Impressionist became a standing joke, penetrating even to the music-hall stage, and the name Cézanne stood everywhere in artistic circles as synonymous with an inability to draw correctly, a mania for glaring colors inexpertly applied, and a lack of taste in subjects. When Rivière not long afterward wrote an article on Impressionism for *L'Artiste,* he was asked by the editor not to mention Cézanne for fear of annoying the readers.

4

Rivière scarcely exaggerated; after fifteen years of hard work Cézanne remained a laughingstock to all but a few forward-looking minds. The public and most of the painters, advanced as well as academic, rejected his expression of emotion with all the hatred that fear of the unknown arouses; they did not understand, therefore they mocked.

Cézanne's reaction was the reaction of greatness. He did not complain that his difficult struggle to master intensity of feeling had been cruelly misinterpreted. He said nothing. He even admitted to himself that his critics were not without reason. When he told his mother that he believed himself to be the best painter of all around him, he did not speak of the present, but the future. He knew that he had far to go, that extravagances of temperament still marred his work; he suspected that the final advance into maturity had to be made in the southern country of his birth. But he stayed on in Paris, mocked though he was, because he was not yet convinced that Paris had taught him all it had to teach; to learn that, he was prepared to suffer. Prepared but not contented. He said nothing, but his feelings were in any case incommunicable; what was this but a continuation of the old horror of his child- and boyhood? As a man he seemed damned. If this was the price a great painter must pay, he would pay it, but he began to wonder, did the world's injustice extend to this, that the merits of a painter could be submerged by the social failings of the man? Puzzled, hurt, cynical, he withdrew still further into his shell of roughness. But he threw himself into his work with a new fury, a controlled fury. He painted with Guillaumin in the country round Issy, he painted at Chantilly, at Fontainebleau, at Auvers, he painted once more with Pissarro at Pontoise. And at Pontoise he found a new disciple working with Pissarro, Paul Gauguin.

Gauguin, sailor and stockbroker, had met Pissarro a year or two earlier at the house of his godfather, Paul Arosa, banker and patron of the arts. Pissarro had talked so earnestly and so convincingly, backing his talk with pictures by himself and other Impressionists bought by Arosa, that Gauguin also launched into the collecting of contemporary paintings. He bought canvases by Pissarro, Monet, Manet, Renoir, Guillaumin, and Cézanne. Then he was no longer content to buy canvases; he wanted to paint them. He went to night classes, worked hard. By 1876 he had had a painting accepted by the Salon.

This honor that Cézanne had sought for so many years meant nothing to Gauguin the moment it was gained. He knew well enough that the accepted painting was conventional and could have been made by a dozen men. He studied again and again the Impressionist canvases of his collection, tried to reproduce them and, feeling an instinctive sympathy with them, put himself into the hands of Pissarro during the next summer—the summer of 1877.

The meeting between himself and Cézanne was momentous, for it was the meeting of two of the three great Post-Impressionists. To Gauguin it was momentous, in fact and at that moment, for of all the Impressionists he most admired Cézanne. To Cézanne he appeared no more than a talented Sunday painter, rather free with his tongue. The three men went out painting together. All were tall and strong. Pissarro, waving beard and hair now white, looked older than his forty-seven years. Cézanne was as strong and vigorous as the twenty-nine-year-old Gauguin, but his black hair had shrunk to the sides and back of his head; the pate was completely bald; few would dream that he was still two years short of his fortieth birthday.

Cézanne was not one to crawl to a man, or even to be agreeable if he did not feel like it, just because that man had bought his paintings and might, properly handled, buy more. The fact prejudiced him slightly in Gauguin's favor, and that is the most that can be said. And before the summer was out even this had given way to bitterness. A Salon exhibitor—this amateur, this Sunday painter who openly sought guidance from Pissarro and himself! No, that was too much. He could scarcely look at the breezy young man without dislike.

CHAPTER ELEVEN

Father and Son

1878–1879

CÉZANNE came down to Aix at the beginning of 1878 and ran straight into trouble with his father. The trouble was a very real one to him; to those who read about it in his letters and elsewhere it is with some difficulty seen as anything but a long-drawn-out continuation of the farce of seven years earlier. Nor is this merely the reaction of an onlooker many years later; the sense of farce is heightened by the certainty that old M. Cézanne never had the slightest intention of disowning his son.

The obvious is always least obvious to those on the spot. To Cézanne, discovery by his father of Hortense and young Paul spelled instant disaster: the end of his allowance; the beginning of a lifetime of shifts to earn money, where and how he did not know and could not imagine; the end of the painter.

So the round of precautions continued, Cézanne abetted by his mother as before. It was his mother, again at her apartment at L'Estaque, whom he asked to find him rooms at Marseilles, cheap "but in a district where there is not too much murdering"—a nice touch of humor recalling a Cézanne too often forgotten. The request was

made, to avoid the curiosity of old M. Cézanne, through
the rapidly prospering Zola, who, following his friend's
recommendation, was spending the summer of 1877 at
L'Estaque. It proved to be premature; autumn in the
countryside around Paris was irresistible to a painter
just feeling his true power. Cézanne stayed on. Not until
January did he move.

For the next fifteen months he lived a nomadic existence, oscillating harassedly between Marseilles, where
he had settled Hortense and his son, L'Estaque with his
mother, and the Jas de Bouffan where he worked furiously
in the top floor studio into which no member of the family
was allowed to set foot—a restriction notably observed
by his father.

Old Monsieur Cézanne watched these uneasy comings
and goings with a sardonic eye. He watched the post too,
and by March Cézanne was appealing agitatedly to Zola
to find him a job and to reply via the *poste restante* at
Aix. "The situation between my father and me has become very greatly strained," he said, "and I am threatened
with the loss of my entire allowance. A letter written to
me by Monsieur Chocquet in which he spoke of 'Madame
Cézanne and little Paul' has clearly revealed my position
to my father, who was already on the lookout, filled
with suspicions, and who had nothing better to do than
open and read a letter sent to me although it was addressed to *Mons. Paul Cézanne, artiste peintre.*"

Zola sympathized but advised caution—he no doubt
foresaw more clearly than his temperamental friend the
quick end to any situation he might find him—and
Cézanne obeyed. His son became ill, he rushed to Marseilles and, unable to get home to dinner by train, walked
the twenty miles so that the old man should have nothing
to reproach him with. He did not walk fast enough; he

was an hour late. But even had he been in time he could not avoid a reckoning. Monsieur Cézanne, who had his own sense of humor, had taken to bearding Paul's acquaintances in the street. One day he buttonholed Villevieille (then teaching in Aix) with a demand for congratulations and, to the open-mouthed painter's mute enquiry, an explanatory "I'm a grandfather, you know!" And he answered Villevieille's astonished "Paul's not married!" with an ironic "He's been seen coming out of a toyshop with a rocking horse and other things. You're not going to tell me that they're for himself?"

These efforts to force his son into the open drove the alarmed Cézanne deeper into prevarication and widened the unfortunate misunderstanding between the two men. The sympathetic—and surely slightly amused—Zola soon received, after a "I am taking every precaution to prevent my father from getting hold of definite proofs," an appeal for sixty francs to be sent direct to Hortense at Marseilles.

His allowance had been cut by half. Old Monsieur Cézanne was not angry or mean, as his son imagined, he was disgusted and hurt by his son's lack of trust. Cézanne was then in his fortieth year. He had sold less than fifteen pictures in fifteen years of painting, he showed no sign of making money or a name; on the contrary, from his father's reading of the newspapers, from his son's angry asides and the tittle-tattle of Aix, it was only too clear that he had made himself and his work a laughingstock in Paris. All this, so uncongenial to the proud old man, he dismissed; he kept his regrets to himself. But lack of honesty was another matter; his son was lying and he knew it; he was not even lying well, any fool could tell when Paul Cézanne was ill at ease.

So Monsieur Cézanne punished him in characteristic fashion. He had allowed him 200 francs a month in Paris.

But what did he want with 200 francs while he spent his time between his father's home at Aix and his mother's apartment at L'Estaque, and when he swore and declared that he remained a single man without any encumbrances?

Cézanne's version, to Zola, of the culmination of several unhappy conversations in the Jas de Bouffan was, naturally, different. "In defiance of the sanctity of treaties I've only been able to get 100 francs from my father. I actually feared he would give me nothing at all. He hears from a number of people that I have a child and tries to catch me out in every possible way. He would like to take it off my hands, he says. . . ."

Zola sent the money. For five months in succession the worried Cézanne, dodging from father to mother, from mother to Hortense and the child, with many a backward glance appealed to Zola for news and help—the news to be sent to Monsieur A. Fiquet at L'Estaque, his precautions extending as far as a pseudonym. Zola sent the news and paid Hortense promptly every time. He also received Paul's sole confidences with steadying words. The two men had little enough in common by this time, but an alliance against Monsieur Cézanne never failed.

Occasionally, as in the past, Zola's wholeheartedness in the campaign echoed uneasily in his friend's conscience. He tried once or twice, half-heartedly, to assuage the pang. "It would take too long to explain the good man to you," he said, "but with him appearances are deceptive." And again: "My good family, first-rate in many ways it must be admitted, is perhaps a bit miserly with a wretched painter who has never been able to cope, but this is a slight oddity, easily excusable in the provinces."

Two months after this, toward the end of July, came another contretemps which swayed Cézanne back into anger. The man with whom he had left his keys in Paris had rented his rooms to visitors to the Exposition of that year. The owner of the apartment discovered this, thought that Cézanne was privy to it, and wrote with his quarterly receipt "a pretty stiff letter, complaining that my apartment was occupied by strangers. My father read the aforementioned letter and inferred that I was concealing women in Paris. This is beginning to take on the air of a vaudeville sketch. . . ."

Six weeks later Hortense's father wrote to her at the Paris apartment. The landlord sent on the letter—addressed to Mme Cézanne—to the Jas de Bouffan. Paul was at L'Estaque, his father opened the letter and confronted him with it when he returned: the triumphant smile can be imagined. "I denied everything violently," Cézanne told Zola, "and as, most luckily, the name Hortense wasn't mentioned in the letter, I insisted that it was addressed to some other woman of the same name."

This explanation was so preposterous that M. Cézanne's sense of humor got the better of his annoyance; he rewarded the unskillful romancer with the sum of 300 francs. "Incredible," exclaimed the gratified but bewildered Cézanne. The true reason being as far beyond him as a true reading of his father's character, he found another. "I believe he's been giving the glad eye to a charming little maid we have at Aix: my mother and I are at L'Estaque." M. Cézanne was then in his eighty-first year.

2 ~~~~

This unexpected windfall brightened the autumn of a dark year. Cézanne's troubles were not wholly financial; moving about as he did, sleeping with Hortense at Marseilles whenever he could get away from L'Estaque for the night, frequently spending would-be conciliatory days

at the Jas de Bouffan, his work suffered. He did little and
that little could not satisfy a critical sense growing severer
with every year that passed.

Nor was this all. Everything being known in Aix, or
imagined when not known, stories of the strife between
father and son, of Cézanne's women and children in
various corners of France, ran over town like wildfire.
Cézanne had never been a popular figure in Aix—his
straight talk and the way he dressed offended the conventional townsfolk—and his early experiences at cafés
began to repeat themselves. He had now to answer for
his painting, too. He never spoke of it, never showed it,
but the town gossips were content to denigrate without
physical evidence. Rumors of the scenes at the Impressionist exhibitions had come south, gaining accretions
on the way, and one or two Aixois—Gilbert, for example,
—had been allowed to examine Cézanne's work. Cézanne
had laughed at Gilbert's horrified reaction and had praised
the man. Gilbert did not return the compliment, nor did
Villevieille, once one of his prize pupils.

So Cézanne is soon telling Zola, "Villevieille's pupils jeer
at me when I pass." But like all great men, incapable of
pettiness, essentially simple, looking first always to a
possible shortcoming in himself, he did not blackguard
the boys as a lesser man would have done. He continues
naïvely but lovably: "I must get my hair cut. Perhaps it
is too long."

He was, however, understandably glad to be out of
Aix; and in November he had the rare pleasure of looking after the six-year-old Paul at L'Estaque for a month.
Hortense had to pay an urgent visit to Paris to see her
ailing father—Guillaumin found her a room near him
in Rue de Vaugirard—and Cézanne, begging Zola to
send her 100 francs, took charge of the child. He doted

on the boy, who, he told Chocquet proudly, "is a terror
in every way and is going to give us plenty of trouble in
the future." He used the little Paul as model time after
time. His pleasure in having him to himself was clouded
only by the fear which had blighted the year: "my father
might have caught us unawares. One could almost think
there was a conspiracy to reveal my situation to him—
even my little bastard of a landlord is chipping in."

Cézanne's passion for his child, natural enough in a
lonely, self-repressed man, was particularly revealing because the boy was the image of his mother, in looks and
in disposition. Like so many women who join their lives
to great artists, Hortense is completely overshadowed by
Cézanne. She is scarcely ever heard of; she gave him what
he wanted as far as she was able; and can best be judged
by the change in his work. For the rest she can be seen
in her son—a practical, hard-working, capable, undemon-
strative man. This son was to show distinct resemblances
to his paternal grandfather, resemblances which explain
the basic reason for Cézanne's choice of woman. A man
who is governed from birth till death by parental influence cannot escape that influence by putting space between it and himself. If he runs, he runs in a circle;
that influence has become a need, and he will search for
its like without knowing what he does. Hence Hortense;
for there was in her, as in her son, beyond the obvious
attraction of sex, a hard-headed strength of character
reminiscent of Louis-Auguste. Very occasionally, women
like Hortense reveal themselves for a moment before
withdrawing into obscurity, and provide further indica-
tions for the choice of the man. Hortense did so at this
time. Years earlier, when she first met Cézanne, she had
also met a friend of his from the Aix Academy, the
deformed painter Achille Emperaire. Cézanne made a

portrait of him which is now well known—one of the best of his early works—liked him, and helped him. For Emperaire was consistently unsuccessful, perpetually in want, and Cézanne, always moved by life's failures, showed with him the exceptionally kind heart so often hidden by rough manners. Hortense also liked Emperaire; she also was kind. She was practical too. So this autumn, while Cézanne wrote to his universal provider, Zola, to enlist his sympathies (neither the first nor last appeal of this kind), Hortense, risking discovery and unpleasantness, went over to Aix to visit Emperaire, his wife, and his three small children, all half-starving, to bring them food and clothing and comfort.

It is no matter for wonder that Cézanne, writing to Chocquet early the next year (both the Chocquets knew and were fond of Hortense) speaks affectionately and proudly of "My wife." She, he says, paying a compliment in his own inimitable fashion, "who is responsible for providing our daily food and who knows what a worry and annoyance it can be, shares in the torments of Madame Chocquet and sends her most respectful greetings."

CHAPTER TWELVE

The Outsider

1879–1880

FOR the next year, from the spring of 1879 to the spring of 1880, Cézanne settled with Hortense and the child in a district new to him, the town of Melun, thirty miles south of Paris.

Despite all the alarms and excursions of the previous year he had left Aix on good terms with his father and with his full allowance restored. "I had hoped," he told Zola from L'Estaque before leaving, "to experience a taste of complete peace here, but on the contrary I have been more than ever harassed because of the lack of understanding between me and the parental authority." And he continued in a like strain of unreality: "The author of my days is obessed by the thought of freeing me. There's only one good way of doing that, and that's to stick on another two or three thousand francs per year, not to wait until I'm dead to make me his heir—for I'm sure I shall die before him."

This did not mean, as Zola naturally interpreted it, that he wished for his father's death. But, illogically, he longed for freedom from the role of deceiver. To some men duplicity comes naturally; to Cézanne, forced, as he thought, to use it from his earliest days, it was a form of torture; he did not like it and he was no good at it.

Apparently he never once thought that the best way to get a bigger allowance was to put all his cards on the table. The kind of twisted caution that his nature and up-bringing had fathered on him restricted him to 200 francs a month. He did not see it that way. He was as astonished by the resumption of the 200 francs as he had been by the gift of 300, and was dissatisfied into the bargain. The key to his father's regard was to descend with him into the grave.

But at least Cézanne was free to live once more with Hortense and his son without serious money worries, and to paint. He did, however, regard himself as in a sense exiled from the source of his painting's power; not for another two and a half years was he to visit Aix, and much though he painted in the interval, and well, he knew in the back of his mind that only Aix and the south could bring to light the great painter. Not for years, never since he had gained command of technique and control of emotion, had he been able to work in Aix with carefree spirit; the differences with his father poisoned contentment and kept the painter confined.

To this extent his fulfillment of himself as man by his meeting with Hortense hampered his fulfillment as painter. But he did not brood over it; he was a slow, methodical worker, he was faced with the fascination of innumerable new motifs. He also had a momentous decision to make.

The Impressionists had hoped to organize their fourth show in the previous year. Cézanne had been invited to exhibit and had told Zola to loan them a still life. The exhibition was postponed until the following year, 1879, and it was generally assumed that he would again send some canvases. But something had happened in the interim which made him hesitate. Guillemet, long since turned into a "respectable" painter, had been elected to the Jury of the 1879 Salon.

Cézanne's quandary was very real. If he tried to exhibit at the Salon he could not expect to be exhibited by the Impressionists. If he did not try to exhibit at the Salon that year, he would miss perhaps his only chance of being admitted, of impressing and pleasing his father, and of improving his financial future. Though he had seen little of Guillemet in recent years, there had been no open break and he reckoned that his old acquaintance's memories of hospitality and happy days at Aix would come to his rescue. Against this he had never forgotten many kindnesses of Pissarro, the leading spirit of the Impressionist exhibition, and knew himself to be the most rebellious of the rebels among whom he was expected to take his stand. How could he fail to exhibit without ingratitude and self-betrayal?

The issue was decided, in what degree cannot be said, by two facts: by his feeling for his father and by his remembrance of the treatment his canvases had received at the two Impressionist exhibitions. Was it not true that the Impressionists would fare better without him, that his work jeopardized the chances of all?

With this typically self-doubting thought riding side by side with an insistent query—was he really a true Impressionist?—and a powerful emotional impulse, he made his decision; a decision which he announced to Pissarro in equally typical fashion: "I think that amid all the difficulties raised by my sending to the Salon it would be most becoming in me not to take part in the Impressionist Exhibition."

At the same time he went to see Guillemet, who

promised to put in a good word for him. As he did, but
without effect: he was rejected again.

No longer one of the Impressionists, rejected by the
Salon, he was now isolated. He remained on good terms
with the Impressionists he had known well, Pissarro,
Monet, and Renoir, but with the possible exception of
Pissarro they were more relieved than hurt to have him
outside the movement; his reputation as the wild man
of modern painting did harm to Impressionism, they
thought, as long as he called himself one of them.
Nevertheless he was isolated. He had cut himself off
from the one positive avenue to future fame and profit.
His work could still be seen at Tanguy's, but as no one but
painters ever went there and no one was shown his
canvases unless asked for, the chance of making sales
or exerting an influence was remote. With two negligible
exceptions he was to remain for the next sixteen years
as one dead to the world of painting.

2 ⬿

Melun was not, as now, a dormitory for Paris businessmen, but a charming old town on the Seine. Cézanne
painted well there and, because of an exceptionally hard
winter, made one of his rare snowscapes. He painted
at Zola's too; for Zola, making money hand over fist
with one startling novel after another, had bought a house
at Médan on the Seine west of Paris. There went Cézanne, sometimes inviting himself (a notable sign of
absolute trust in his friend) and, doing his best to avoid
the gay and clever crowds which Zola assembled, painting in the garden by the river, on the river, and in the
lush countryside. He was not an easy guest. He was

hopelessly messy to have in the house, covered with spots and splashes of paint from beard to waistcoat; anything he touched was liable to become uncleanable. He would stump out of the room without a word when conversation became too loud or too flippant for him. When interrupted at work he would break off in a fury. When Guillemet, for instance, sauntered into the garden where he was making a portrait of Mme Zola and chattered to the model, Cézanne slashed a hole in the canvas with his palette knife, snapped his brushes in two, walked away, and caught the next train home.

These anecdotes of the temperamental painter—and there are dozens of them—were bandied about Paris and have been repeated ever since. But repetition without commentary is mere gossip and as malicious. Cézanne could have been excused for behaving badly before the literary smart set of Zola's country house, even if only because it was expected of him; he was universally regarded as a showpiece, the mad painter in person. But there was a better reason. He was one of those who could do nothing easily; from the raising of a hand in salute to the writing of a letter, every action was an effort, an effort unimaginable to all except the unlucky thousands who through no fault of their own are thrown on the world physically, mentally, and emotionally clumsy.

Of all actions, painting came the most hard to him. When he sat himself before an easel he was bedeviled by every possible disadvantage. Worst of all was the need to discipline the fiery spirit which, given half a chance, would wreck every work he undertook. Gritting his teeth, he restrained the man who, like Van Gogh, would splash the paint on centimeters thick and be done with the canvas in a few hours. For him, that was not the way of truth of vision or feeling; the way, for him, was the grinding labor of forcing tumultuous emotion into a form that would at once contain and fully express it. Deliberately he painted slowly, adding one small dab or brush stroke to another. For hours he would do nothing but study the motif before him, absorbing its atmosphere, analyzing the play of light and color, pondering the best means to express the exact nuance of every shade. He did violence to the man but step by slow step was liberating the artist. Everything had to give way to this sustained effort of imagination and will: time was nothing, people did not exist, tidiness and cleanliness were abstractions invented by a supposedly civilized world.

Hence his fury when brought back to life by a model who shifted position, a Guillemet in search of distraction. The model's movement, the chat of Guillemet, harmless to them, were tragedies to Cézanne. They broke the concentration, destroyed the discipline, ruined the rapport between eye and brain and subject. Other, more fortunate, men could recover their poise quickly because they had made less effort to acquire it. For Cézanne the day was lost and perhaps the painting, too. He who at twenty-two had smashed a portrait of Zola because it fell short of the standard he demanded of himself was unlikely to be less critical in his forties, and he was not; he worked to a harsh rule, destroying what he made again and again.

The men and women who visited Zola's country house could not be expected to understand these inner compulsions, inner tortures. Like most people in the world they accepted everything at face value. Cézanne, to them, was acting precisely as they hoped, up to his reputation. Why ask why? And when Zola's wife gave the painter piles of old rags in the hope that he would

wipe himself clean every time a spot of paint spat onto
his face or clothes, she had no idea of the futility of
such an apparently practical gesture. He thanked her
gruffly, took the rags, forgot or dirtied them, and remained his incorrigible, uncorruptible self.

Zola alone might have understood him. To a point he
did. Yet he had little or no faith in the painter; he
thought that Cézanne had missed his way and would
never find it; he believed that his old friend's temperamental defects, which had clung to him into middle
age and would obviously never leave him, barred the way
to self-knowledge and self-expression.

As his life and work showed, Zola did not possess deep
feelings; his enthusiasms could and did pass as depth
of feeling at the time, but contemporary judgment then
as always was swayed by outward appearance. In this
he fitted the role. Like so many fundamentally cold men
he was exuberant, friendly, open. Like so many vain
men he made generous gestures when flattered. And
Cézanne did flatter him by his confidence, his assumption that this friend alone understood him. For the past
twenty years, to put it no earlier, Zola had seen himself romantically in the role of Cézanne's savior, fighting
an endless duel with Monsieur Cézanne for the soul of
his son. By what Cézanne told him he believed that he
had won the fight. Jubilant, he typically and purposely
overlooked the fact that he had long since given up
the fight and that it had been transferred to Cézanne's
loving imagination. In the old days he had had an inkling
of what lay behind the rages and despairs of his friend.
He had proclaimed him far and wide as a budding
genius. By the early eighties, when this friend was able
to visit him frequently, these displays of temperament
had assumed a very different aspect in his mind; they
were at once an appeal to pity from a failure, a show

sometimes embarrassing but more often titivating for
his many visitors, and above all they provided him with
magnificent copy for the novel which he hoped would
prove his magnum opus. The notes on Cézanne, his looks,
his behavior, multiplied in the source book which Zola
kept at Médan.

To all of this Cézanne remained blind. He loved seldom
but with a passion. Like all men driven by nature and
circumstance to suspicion, he was least suspicious when
once he had given his heart. He knew that Zola was
disappointed in his work, but with the humility of the
great he accepted it. Was not he himself still struggling
to find the way? How then, could he expect his friend to
praise the canvases which expressed these struggles? On
the contrary he generously gave Zola credit for critical
integrity; his friend's attitude seemed to him admirable
and exemplary, a refusal to allow personal feeling to sway
artistic judgment.

Yet in these years when he clung to Zola as he had
never clung since the days of boyhood excursions about
Aix, some hint of the future must have stirred in his
subconscious. He allowed himself to make what for
him, who used a pen with such difficulty, were passionate
appeals to past loyalty and love. So, soon after explaining apologetically, "I am still straining every nerve to
find my way as a painter," he wrote significantly, "I
remain gratefully your old friend of schooldays." And
again: "Heartfelt greetings from the Provençal in whom
maturity has not preceded old age."

Significant words indeed from such a man. Somewhere,
somehow he dreaded what it was impossible to suspect
from one who, he meekly and thankfully wrote, "still
consents to remain my friend." He could not dream how
soon and how thoroughly that friend was to strike the
blow which was to shatter his life.

CHAPTER THIRTEEN

Toward the Salon

1880–1882

ZOLA's true sentiments soon began to declare themselves. After his year at Melun, Cézanne, restless as always when long away from the south, moved into the outskirts of Paris, to the district known as Plaisance. He and his little family lived for a year at 32 Rue de l'Ouest, a few doors from lodgings he had occupied three years earlier.

From here he "flew" to the fifth Impressionist exhibition where he ran into Alexis and Dr. Gachet and, at the doctor's insistence, into one of his rare dinner engagements. He also met Monet and Renoir. They asked him to enlist Zola's help. Both had abandoned this Impressionist show in favor of a return to the Salon, but their works had been so badly hung there that they protested to the Minister of Fine Arts. They asked Zola through Cézanne to print this letter in the newspaper he was then associated with, *Le Voltaire.*

Zola agreed. He was always willing to help old friends and still more willing to help himself by helping them. Famous as he had become, hatred and admiration each playing its part in his notoriety, a public word from him would arouse notice and discussion throughout Paris.

154

So he did not merely print the letter, but commented on it in four long articles, taking with one hand what he gave with the other. Like the Irishman, he was "agin the government"; authority, convention, taste, habit, he deplored and fought them all. The Salon was an old bogey; he struck out at it fiercely.

Less happily, he chose to examine the work of the Impressionists and to forecast the future of the movement. A fanatical defender of apparently lost causes does not often make the most judicious critic. Zola's pontifical judgments were absurdly far from the mark. After describing Impressionism as "the only possible evolution" of painting, he deplored the fact that "not one painter in this group has applied the new formula powerfully and definitely . . . we look vainly for the masterpiece which will set the seal on the formula . . . they remain unequal to their self-ordained task, they stammer, unable to find the right word."

In his vanity Zola had gone over unwittingly to the side of the enemy; his praise elsewhere of Pissarro, Monet, Renoir was cancelled out by this arbitrary limitation of their achievements. He could not see the significance of what he looked at, and his vision was densest when he looked at the work of his lifelong friend. Cézanne, he declared in these articles, had "the temperament of a great painter, but is still wrestling with technical difficulties."

This backhanded compliment placed his friend among the laggards of the Impressionists. It blithely ignored the fact, which would have been obvious to any real critic who knew Cézanne and his work, that through him another evolution of painting was not only possible but probable. The bones of it were there to the seeing eye. Zola missed the opportunity of opportunities—the hailing of the birth of Post-Impressionism. Yet Cézanne remained simply grateful for what his friend had done, and wrote from the heart to tell him so. He missed the truth behind these public reservations because such a truth was not conceivable to him; his trust in Zola was complete.

2 ~~~~~

He was rejected again at the Salon of 1880 and again in 1881. This continuation of the unbroken series of rejections—he had first submitted work eighteen years earlier—drove him out of Paris. In the spring of 1881 he returned to Pissarro at Pontoise and stayed there painting with him until the late autumn. Pissarro was balm to his spirit, bearing no ill will for the break from Impressionism proper, manifesting a heartening and self-less admiration for his work.

Gauguin was not always balm to his spirit. For Gauguin was there again, spending his summer holidays at his easel by the side of Pissarro. This was a Gauguin much changed from the amateur of a few years past. He still worked at the Bourse, he remained in theory a Sunday painter, but his painting and his view of painting had advanced; he was giving all his spare time to it and had already begun to think of throwing up his job and becoming a professional painter. This last, because his second appearance at an Impressionist exhibition, in April of that year, had provided one of the triumphs of the show. His work was in fact derivative—he had been leaning too heavily on Pissarro—but in one picture he broke away at a bound into naturalism of a most striking and original kind. J. K. Huysmans, one of Zola's

friends whom Cézanne had met at Médan, claimed
publicly that this was one of the greatest nudes ever
painted.

So the Gauguin who painted side by side with Cézanne
and Pissarro during that summer of 1881 was no longer
a beginner, but a painter to be reckoned with. He was
no less deferential to Cézanne than before, but it was the
deference of a man who was beginning to know why
he liked what he liked.

Cézanne, always liable to touchiness when with any
but the oldest of acquaintances, found Gauguin's complete freedom from inhibitions hard to bear. Gauguin
said what he thought in plain words. He had more to
say this time, as befitted a painter who was getting into
his stride. Looking at the arrogant profile and listening
to the authoritative voice, Cézanne found himself in
an unfamiliar dilemma. Here was an admirer, that rare
thing in his life. He could not doubt Gauguin's sincerity
in that. But did he want such an admirer? he was soon
asking himself. Gauguin swore as though he were throwing off a momentary irritation, not as though he were
covering some unspeakable thought. He drank with the
healthy satisfaction of the man with a large thirst, not
with the desperation of the man who wanted to forget an
ungrateful world. His manner with women was un-
believably free. He sauntered about, long legs firmly
planted, head up as though he owned the world, as
though he had never known what it was to avert an
eye. To a repressed Puritan with a passionate nature,
this openly sensuous man, taking an unconscious pride
in his virility, provided a source of constant offense. The
offense—outrage would scarcely be too strong a word—
as usual worked itself out sideways. Cézanne began to

wonder whether Gauguin was insincere in another way, whether that masterful *cum* hail-fellow-well-met attitude, so antipathetic to him, covered a lack of originality.

Such a thought once admitted could only lead to mis-understanding. Old suspicions sprang up. Cézanne could see at a glance the influence of Pissarro in Gauguin's work. Now the fellow was following him about! His next pictures would no doubt be pseudo Cézannes. He could see the resemblance already. Unlike Pissarro, who took imitation as a compliment, Cézanne regarded it as a crime. He had not his friend's sweetness of nature. But again, Pissarro had escaped his own long years of struggle to express himself, a struggle not yet done.

Cézanne was not sorry to see the end of Gauguin's holiday. Gauguin gone, the grudge would soon have gone, too. Unhappily Pissarro had a weakness; he liked a good gossip and could not always deny himself the pleasure of passing on the unpassable. In his bread and butter letter Gauguin said lightly, "Has Monsieur Cézanne found the exact *formula* for a work acceptable to every-one? If he discovers the recipe for compressing the ex-aggerated expression of his 'sensations' into a single, unique procedure, please try to make him talk in his sleep by administering one of those mysterious homeopathic drugs, and come to Paris as soon as possible to tell us all about it."

Pissarro showed this letter to Cézanne. That was enough to elevate Gauguin into the master thief. The emotional Cézanne saw his years of labor thrown away, snatched up by this immoral businessman of a Gauguin. Years later, when Gauguin's work had won a large au-dience, Cézanne's suspicions were to burst into the open accusation that Gauguin had stolen *"ma petite sensation,"* into shouts of "Don't talk to me about Gauguin! I'd like to wring the fellow's neck!" The accusation was understandable but mistaken. Gauguin was influenced by Cézanne because Cézanne alone of all men then painting expressed his emotions somewhat as Gauguin, had he possessed the technical skill, would have expressed them; in their reaction to nature the two men, the extrovert Gauguin and the closed Cézanne, were curiously alike, and their "sensations" were bound to be related. But Cézanne could never see this; he had struggled too hard and too long.

3

This year, Duranty having died, his novel appeared posthumously. There was good reason for this; the book was filled with libelous portraits of which Cézanne's was the most prominent. Duranty, who had a sharp tongue, had regarded Cézanne's behavior and appearance at the Guerbois and Nouvelle-Athènes with sarcastic asides. A friend of Manet, he did not care for Cézanne's hostility. Like Manet, something of a dandy, he was shocked by the sight of Cézanne shambling in straight from his studio. With Manet he was anxious to show that modernity did not mean antisocial behavior, that the advanced painter could take his place in the fashionable Salon. "Dangerous demonstrations," he called these paint-spattered visitations. And though Cézanne's attendance at the cafés fell away markedly after the savage treatment of his entries to the first and third Impressionist exhibitions, Duranty had already marked him down as the perfect vehicle for an attack on the painter who insisted on looking like a painter and behaving like a genius.

An extract from a visit to the painter's studio shows what he thought of Cézanne—Maillobert in his novel.

"I knocked. 'Enter!' shouted a voice with a most peculiar accent. No sooner had I got in than I told myself, 'I have come to see a madman!' . . . The painter, bald and with an enormous beard . . . appearing at once youthful and ancient, was a kind of symbolic divinity of the studio—indescribably sordid. He bowed deeply with a smile both idiotic and sly. All the time my eyes were blattered by the enormous canvases filling the studio and painted in such frightful colors that I was petrified. 'Ah ha!' cried Maillobert, exaggerating the nasal drawl of the Marseillais. 'Monsieur is a connoisseur of painting?' He pointed to the vast canvases: 'Here are a few little daubs from my palette.' . . . A number of portraits caught my attention, portraits without faces for the heads were a mass of spots. . . .

"Two of his friends turned up, bearded, black, filthy. 'Perhaps he's the master of the chimney-sweep school,' I thought. His friends regarded the master's works as though they had never seen them before. 'What strength! What boldness!' they exclaimed. 'Compared with this, Courbet and Manet are so much chaff!' Maillobert, smiled, gratified, dug a spoon in one of his chemist's pots and brought out a hefty trowelful of green. He plastered it onto a canvas bearing a few lines indicating a landscape. He juggled the spoon about for a bit, and I could see that what he had smeared on might with a great effort just be taken to represent a field. I noticed that the color on all his canvases was about half an inch thick and formed hills and valleys in relief. . . ."

This was puerile, like the entire book, and deserved Cézanne's silent contempt. Nonetheless it did, in exaggerated form, explain the manner in which he was coming to be regarded. To speak of Cézanne's withdrawal from the world is to suggest an obliteration that is nonsense. No gifted painter in France could ever completely hide his light under a bushel. Cézanne certainly could not; his intimacy with Zola and the championship of Pissarro, Dr. Gachet, and Chocquet made sure that he was mentioned from time to time. But he and his work were so seldom seen that, since Paris insists on thinking something about everything, what was not known had to be invented. Or if not invented, built on the slenderest of foundations. So, easily, inevitably, Cézanne became the wild beast of modern painting, ferocious to meet, ferocious on his canvases. It was the kind of legend which if not true ought to be true; the cafés lapped it up, the salons elaborated it; this was precisely the *frisson* so beloved of the Parisians and they made the most of it.

Cézanne remained silent. Inwardly he raged. Disgust with Paris rose once more and engulfed him. Aix, difficult though it was, was better than this. Suddenly, in November, 1881, he returned there.

4 〰

His stay in the south was to be shorter than he thought. But this time it was not interrupted as before by fear of his father's investigations discovering the truth. He found old Monsieur Cézanne beginning slowly to break up. No trouble there, and no reduction of his allowance. He soon went off to L'Estaque where he hoped to settle in peace to a renewed attempt to work a way through to his "sensation."

Peace evaded him. Renoir, seduced by Cézanne's enthusiasm, arrived at L'Estaque to paint. Ever since Chocquet had taken up Cézanne with such gusto, Renoir had looked kindly on him. Lowly born himself, he accepted Cézanne's exaggerated peasant's accent and manner with no more than a grimace aside. He even painted his portrait. The men were far from intimate, met seldom, but respected each other. They had one aim in common at least, an unbroken belief in the advantages of showing at the Salon.

"We are going to work together," announced Renoir to Durand-Ruel, perhaps a shade optimistically, for there was little chance of Cézanne accepting for long without outburst his companion's somewhat sentimental view of nature.

But Cézanne was not put to the test. He was soon occupied in another fashion. Despite his praise of "the mild sun without wind," Renoir went down with a bad chill after a few weeks of painting in the open—painting and walking, for Cézanne was tough, tireless.

Cézanne at once revealed an unsuspected side to his nature. He looked after Renoir with rough tenderness and, helped by his mother, who had come over to be near him, nursed him back to health. "I can't tell you how good Cézanne has been," Renoir exclaimed. And he burst into an ecstasy over the cooking of old Mme Cézanne: "the ambrosia of the gods; one should eat and die!"

He did not die but recovered rapidly. But before Cézanne could concentrate his attention fully on his work once more, news came from Paris which sent him hurrying back. He had been accepted at the Salon.

This triumph after nineteen years of unsuccessful trial was about as untriumphal as could possibly be. It was the result of pressure on Guillemet, again on the selection committee, by both Zola and Cézanne. "Paul is still counting on you," Zola had reminded his friend more than a year earlier. And it was made possible only by a favor granted by the Salon to the members of the jury, that each should have the privilege of nominating one work without submitting it to the other members. A condition was attached. This work, accepted by the Salon "out of charity," must be painted by a pupil of the nominator.

So after nineteen years Cézanne was hung (very badly) in the Salon as a pupil of Guillemet, whose work he despised. And the exhibit, a portrait of his uncle, was noted patronizingly by the only critic to catch sight of it as the work of a promising young man who might in the course of time do quite well: "a colorist in embryo," he remarked.

Impossible to imagine jubilation in the heart of the forty-three-year-old Cézanne: easy to imagine the rage of injured pride. Yet this would be to misunderstand the man, his strong underground sense of humor, his feeling for his father. For the old man lived still and at last and not too late his son hoped to justify himself in his eyes.

Hastily he passed the news on. For his part, he could not tear himself from Paris while the Salon was on. Nor could he bring himself to leave afterward. For once the Midi called him in vain. In his simplicity he could not quite believe that a Salon painter could be utterly ignored. And when, by the autumn, the cold truth had been demonstrated to him, he went back to Aix without trace of bitterness: Hortense loved Paris and little Paul loved what she loved; when he was there their pleasure was complete; the stay had not been wasted. Besides to such a man as Cézanne a triumph did not harm for the keeping. After staying with Zola at Médan for the month of September, he returned home to his reward.

CHAPTER FOURTEEN

Calm Before Storm

1882–1884

FOR the next two and a half years he worked peacefully and fruitfully in the south. He did not leave the Jas de Bouffan for more than six months, an unbroken stay which told its own story. His father was no longer diverted from his suspicions by old age, but by gratification. To Louis-Auguste, able to tell every visitor that his son was a Salon painter, Paul had suddenly become an object of pride. His pleasure was not clipped by fine distinctions; Paul spared him details of the manner in which the honor had been gained.

Had Hortense and the boy been there, she and Cézanne would have been saved much suffering and the old man's last years would have been made happier. But although his mother and Marie urged him time and again to tell his father, Cézanne could not bring himself to do so. His reason for silence had shifted privately—he now feared above all to mar the unfamiliar harmony of his relationship with his father. This was as mistaken as his attitude throughout; failing to understand his father to the end, he mistook the resignation of old age for willing submission. The harmony on which he prided

164

himself was too largely enforced by circumstance to approach close to knowledge; the two men remained far apart, old M. Cézanne still resenting his son's lack of trust.

He worked on, however, free from money worries and for some time free from the family attentions which quickly rasped his nerves. He painted several views of the Sainte-Victoire which, seen from the Jas de Bouffan, raised its most impressive side, the triangular end of the 3000-foot ridge soaring spectacularly out of the plain. He was finally driven off by a scene with his sister Rose. She had married the previous year when he, groaning inwardly, went through the "slight trial" of piloting her and her husband through the Paris galleries during their honeymoon. Now she came home for the birth of her child. The child was delicate, the house was in turmoil. Cézanne could hear the raised voices of the three women even in his eyrie in the roof. "All this wasn't very funny," he told Zola. He expressed his feelings with all the vigor of outraged genius, and reported the inevitable with delightful understatement: "I think the result of my outcries is that they won't be coming back."

He took no chances. His nerves, on edge after domestic chaos, prevented him from concentrating on his work. He began to long for his own disciplined home life where, a talkative boy apart, he could work when he wished and as long as he wished and with a perfect model in Hortense, never speaking, never moving for hours on end. Not less passionate as the years passed, he found the celibate life almost unendurable. And in the spring of 1883 an embarrassing event occurred, difficult to explain away to an inquisitive father. The long roll of rejections at the Salon recommenced. Guillemet, willing enough, had had the last prop struck from under his feet; the right to exhibit the work of a pupil was rescinded—rescinded not

improbably because the history of Cézanne's admission
the previous year had become common property.

On every count, a removal seemed wise. Cézanne
rented a small house at L'Estaque, sent for Hortense and
"my terrible youngster," and settled down once more to
try to find himself as painter.

For this after all and above all was the preoccupation
which sooner or later absorbed outside interests. Pissarro,
disturbed by what he saw as stultification of a great talent,
urged him again and again to meet other painters, work
with them, exhibit with them. That way only, he believed,
could a man's work progress. Cézanne refused. Some of
his reasons for refusal have been seen. He also suspected
more and more as time went on that he was fundamentally
out of sympathy with the Impressionists.

Unhappily for him, though coming round to a point of
view which struck at the whole Impressionist technique,
he could not convince himself that he was capable of
making the change, still less of explaining or justifying it.
His chronic lack of self-confidence hampered the emergence of the great painter. This he was to make clear a
few years later when he refuted indignantly the canard
that he did not exhibit with the other moderns because
of "disdain." The reverse was true, emphasized by the public reception of his work. "The many studies I gave myself up to having produced only negative results, and
dreading criticism only too well justified, I made up my
mind to work in silence until the day when I felt myself
capable of defending my attempts in theory as well as in
act."

In silence, therefore, he worked on; a silence broken
only by occasional incomplete explanations or comments
given, ironically enough, to the one man who would be

sure to misunderstand them. The houses at L'Estaque fascinated him; terraced round the little bay, they struck him chiefly as geometrical designs, squares, cubes, oblongs recalling vividly the bared bones of the quarried flank of the Sainte-Victoire. He tells Zola in May that he will not be coming to Paris before the following year: "I am deep in my painting as always."

Four years earlier Zola had commented on the beautiful views at L'Estaque and Cézanne agreed with a rueful "but to reproduce them is scarcely my forte. I began to see nature rather late." Now he was saying, "Yes, I have some beautiful views here but that scarcely makes a *motif*." He had gone far, gone beyond the stage of seeing brilliant colors which, in his youthful passion for startling color, he could not command sufficient technique to apply satisfactorily. Now he had begun to see the Midi as it really is and not with the surface brightness seen by a man of repressed emotions.

Following a brief visit toward the end of the year from Monet and Renoir on their way to Italy, this discovery led, in February of the next year, to a significant exclamation. Cézanne, hearing that Valabrègue was in Aix, went over to see him. Togther they made a round of the countryside, that countryside known so well to the boy Paul. Known so well, yet so superficially, youthful high spirits seeing bright colors which did not exist. Now, in 1884, the man wrote, "My head was full of a conception of this country which seems to me most extraordinary." And this led, toward the end of the year to another cry. He had thought of the shortcomings of modern painting in relation to the country around him, thought of his own shortcomings too. So: "Art is changing dreadfully in the way of external aspect and is taking on most noticeably a small, petty form. At the same time the failure to comprehend harmony is revealing itself more and more in the clash of color and, what is still worse, by the loss of tone."

He was on his way. He could not know, struggling as he was to grasp his "sensation," that only disaster would bring him to his goal.

CHAPTER FIFTEEN

Infatuation

1885–1886

IN the spring of 1885 Cézanne's peaceful existence was abruptly broken. To this day the details of the sudden upheaval remain scanty; the story has to be pieced together from his letters.

What seems to have happened was this. Hortense, longing for Paris and resentful of being kept in perpetual hiding from old M. Cézanne, went north taking her son with her. There was no break. There may have been a quarrel.

Left on his own, Cézanne's hot blood began to get the better of him. In Aix he met a woman, was instantly captivated, and apparently slept with her, though this is far from certain.

Nothing is known about this woman. The only direct reference to her is contained in the fragmentary draft of a letter written by Cézanne on the back of a drawing. "I saw you," he wrote, "and you allowed me to embrace you. From that moment a profound agitation has not stopped disturbing me. You will excuse the liberty, taken by an admirer tormented by anxiety, of writing to you. I don't know how to excuse this liberty, which you may think excessive, but how can I rest under the dejection that weighs me down? Isn't it better to show feeling than hide it? Why, I ask myself, should I say nothing about the cause of my torments? Isn't suffering assuaged when one can express it? And if physical pain seems to feel some relief when the sufferer cries out, isn't it natural, Madame, that unhappy minds seek easement in confession to the adored being?"

This, surely one of the strangest love letters ever written, perfectly expresses the writer. Even in the midst of sexual passion his pen remains unwieldy, he writes with the formality that another man would use toward a complete stranger. The letter also illustrates accurately Cézanne's lifelong difficulty of communication with the outside world. He spoke as he wrote; both speech and writing were powerless to convey the deeply feeling man. In this case an additional element drove him into stiff platitudes—the never-ending conflict of passion and puritanism.

The woman was sufficiently intrigued to begin a correspondence, and this led to the second stage of the affair. Cézanne was engaged to spend the month of June with Renoir at La Roche-Guyon on the Seine west of Paris. Hortense was to join him there. So in the middle of May the first of a number of agitated letters sped off to Zola: "I beg you to do me a service, slight to you, I believe, but enormous to me. This is, to receive some letters addressed to me and to send them on to an address which I will supply you with later on. I am either mad or sensible. *Trahit sua quemque voluptas!*"

A month later, Zola having agreed to the use of his Paris address, Cézanne wrote from Renoir's house begging his friend to send letters to the *poste restante* at La Roche-Guyon.

Three weeks later, he writes, "Life has become rather difficult for me here owing to unforeseen circumstances.

Would you let me know if I can come to your house? If
you haven't yet moved to Médan can you drop me a line?"

The circumstances were unforeseen only by Cézanne.
A worse actor did not exist, as his father had long since
discovered; far from hiding a secret, his face and manner
proclaimed it to the heavens; guilt stared from him.
Hortense discovered, reproached. The painting holiday
with Renoir, from the start an agony of frustration,
turned alarmingly into a series of domestic scenes each
more violent than its predecessor, scenes doubly embarrassing because taking place in another man's house.

Man knows only one remedy: flight. Feverishly Cézanne waited for Zola's reply; wrote again; raged; then
discovered that he had forgotten to ask at the *poste
restante*. Remembering he rushed there with an apologetic
"I'm an absolute fool" to Zola.

Five days later, having had no definite word from
his friend, he could bear the strain no longer. He left for
Villennes, a nearby river village, asking Zola in the same
moment if he could borrow his boat *Nana* to make some
river studies. Zola's silence unnerving him, he begged,
"Don't see my decision as bad. I'm simply obliged to make
a change of scene."

This naïve excuse must have made Zola chuckle. He
could not in any case get in touch with Cézanne at once,
for Villennes was jammed for the July 14 celebrations and
the fleeing man was forced another twenty miles down
river to Vernon, where he found a room.

He did not find peace and, hearing from Zola that he
could not be accommodated at Médan for another week,
burst out with, "I've decided to leave for Aix as soon as
possible. In my present state I can't find an answer here
to my trouble."

Zola, relenting, told him to come to Médan; he was
busy, nearing the end of his latest novel, *L'Œuvre*, and

his wife increasingly found Cézanne more of an embarrassment than pleasure, but the novelist and the friend
Zola were both curious to learn more of the extraordinary
outbreak at Aix and of the scenes at La Roche-Guyon.

Cézanne came, but how much he told his friend and
what that friend's advice was remain, like so much of
this episode, a secret. If Zola tried to dissuade Paul from
returning to Aix he was unsuccessful; by the beginning
of August Cézanne was there again.

By going back to Aix, he had merely changed frying
pan for fire. No peace there. No gratification either. He
found Marie and his mother both fully informed, though
whether by Hortense or local rumor is uncertain. But
the result was the same, a result which the harassed man,
pulled this way and that, described as "the rocks under
my feet which seem to me like mountains."

The womenfolk's frightened appeals—was he mad, to
risk losing Hortense and child, to send his father to the
grave haunted by gossip for once only too true?—had
their effect. "If only I'd had a family which could mind
its own business, everything would have been for the
best!" he exclaimed to Zola toward the end of August.

But though he might write self-deceitfully, his acts
were practical. He gave up the woman and wrote bitterly to Zola of the "comedy" of the past few days and,
as he thought in his easily aroused despair, of the rest
of his life. "I wrote to La Roche-Guyon the same day I
sent you a word of thanks for having thought of me.
Since then, I've had no news; complete isolation for me.
The brothel in town or elsewhere, that's all, nothing more.
I pay cash, the idea isn't pleasant, but I need rest and
must get it whatever the price."

Not for the first time he was saved by his work. All
summer, even in the midst of the one passionate en-

tanglement of his life, he had felt like a lost soul with-out a brush in his hand. "Doing nothing, I am bored to distraction," he told Zola from Renoir's house. Now, his need to avoid the people of Aix drove him into the country. He discovered—rediscovered, to be exact—the picturesque little hill town of Gardanne. The designs formed by the terraced houses built at all angles fasci-nated him as L'Estaque had done before. He spent day after day there sketching and painting and coming back to evening meal at the Jas de Bouffan. And he could soon tell Zola that he was working "fairly free from worry."

The work and the surroundings had their effect. In February of the new year, 1886, he went back to Paris where Hortense and young Paul had gone from La Roche-Guyon. Peace was made. He brought them down with him to Gardanne, Aix being for the moment more than ever impossible. They took rooms, he painted, life began to reassert itself.

"I must tell you," he wrote gratefully to Chocquet, "that I'm painting all the time and that there are many treasures to be wrested from this countryside which has never yet found an interpreter worthy of the riches spread out on every hand." Here was a similar cry to the one he had made two years earlier, after the little tour with Valabrègue. But there was one great difference. "My head was full of a conception of this country," he had written then. Now he had begun to translate this concep-tion into terms of paint on canvas, he had begun his life's work. The recent upheaval served only to turn him to his work with a new passion.

Then in the midst of this renewal of hope and interest, he received from Zola a complimentary copy of *L'Œuvre.*

CHAPTER SIXTEEN

Death of a Man

1886

For years past Zola had sent him every new novel as soon as it was published. Cézanne thanked him punctiliously for each one, read it and tried in a further letter to express his appreciation. These appreciations were rarely enthusiastic. Cézanne, it has been said, was not a literary critic. More to the point, he was not a man to join the throng who raved about Zola's realism; he, blessed or cursed with strong feelings, sensed the lack of them in these novels as in the work of Manet, the painter admired by his friend above all others. He also shrank from the lack of taste shared by the novelist and painter from time to time.

He could not avoid the question, was it literature or journalism, did it come from the head or the heart, this novelty of plain-speaking in the Zola novels? The style, spare, powerful, short-sentenced, fitted the subject no doubt, but was it imposed rather than felt? Nothing in Zola's life could support it. Cézanne had only to think of the house at Médan, luxurious, filled with expensive, tasteless knick-knacks, a house in which the many paintings he had given his friend were not permitted a place on the walls. It was hard for him not to link this with the suggestion of insincerity in the work of the owner of this house.

Even if he managed with an effort to put the house firmly on the shoulders of Madame Zola, a woman who had adapted herself with horrifying ease to her role as wife of a famous author, Zola remained under suspicion. Cézanne's uneasiness in that house, his deliberate flouting of convention (as when he sat himself down to dinner in his painting clothes or took off his jacket when the drawing-room seemed stuffy) were above all an unspoken protest against his friend's ultra-civilized behavior. Similarly with his frequent escapes to paint. For the sight and sound of Zola living up to the great writers of the day who visited Médan was quite shattering to the friend who remained unaffected by the years. Where was the boy who had walked and run and swum and climbed and talked with such infectious, such honest enthusiasm in the Aix countryside thirty years ago? Sadly, Cézanne saw him, not dead—death would at least have had dignity —but overlaid by the successful man of letters.

Loyally he did his best to forget the falling away when he read and tried to judge the Zola novels. He had only to think of Zola's record vis-à-vis himself to be all gratitude. What a record! The years of insistence that he should leave home to paint; the efforts to help him in Paris; the lending and giving of money to Hortense; the helping, on Cézanne's pleas, of Solari, Cabaner, Monet, Renoir; the hospitality at Médan; above all, the very fact of his existence as a sort of repository of hopes and fears—all this spoke of a kindness and generosity in a thousand.

Typically Cézanne forgot or excused the less happy side of the record, the refusal to introduce Duret, the omission of his name in the critical articles, the obvious

loss of faith in him as a painter, the occasional con-
descension at Médan. How, he asked himself, could he
expect Zola or any other man to understand his work
when he remained dissatisfied with it?

Had he been told that Zola and he had nothing in common but boyhood memories, he would have been horrified, disbelieving. His attitude to his friend was summed up perfectly in the exclamation made in the midst
of the emotional turmoil of the previous year. "I am
nothing," he wrote, "and haven't the power to do anything for you, but as I shall die before you I will make
myself useful to you there by interceding with the Most
High for a good place." This from the tongue-tied Cézanne, always fearful of making an exhibition of himself.

Then he read *L'Œuvre*. It was a novel about the painting circles of Paris. Its main character was a man named
Claude Lantier. Lantier was strange, given to violent
rages and peculiar exits and entrances. He dressed in
paint-stained clothes, was fearful of women and unable
to express himself. Nobody understood him or his painting. He believed himself to be a genius, but this belief
was no more than the vanity of a man slightly crazed.
Eventually, ignored by all and failing to sell his work,
he realized that he was a sham and a failure and killed
himself.

The book caused a sensation in Paris as most of Zola's
books had done before it. The painters' cafés buzzed with
talk. The Impressionist painters, most of them caricatured
in the book, recognized Cézanne in Lantier, deplored the
portrait and criticized the writer. He had shown bad
taste, ignorance, and malice, they declared. He had even,
with cruel exactitude, placed Lantier's studio in the very
street where Cézanne had lived eleven years earlier.

Zola, supported by his friends, protested that Cézanne

stood only for the early portrait of Lantier and had
nothing to do with the latter.

All this accusation and defence passed Cézanne by;
he heard little of it and was not interested when he did.
If Zola's excuse reached him he knew what value to put
on it. He had listened to a great deal from Zola at one
time and another about his books, why he wrote them and
how. His principle was, Zola had declared again and
again, to portray men and women as they were and must
become given their particular character, disposition, and
circumstance. That was his special pride; in this honesty
of realism he believed himself to stand alone, to head a
new school of down-to-earth novelists. His argument in
L'Œuvre, logical and pitiless, was that a man like the
early Lantier must end as the later Lantier did, in failure
and suicide. And that, Cézanne realized as he read the
book, was what he really believed. So when Zola said
that the second half of Lantier's life bore no relation to
Cézanne, he was not admitting that he had deliberately
falsified the character, he was admitting that he did not
begin to understand his lifelong friend.

Once or twice in later years Cézanne was reported to
speak harshly of Zola. These reports, like most of the
gossip about Cézanne's eccentricities as he grew old,
have to be taken with much reserve. But one phrase
rings true. "He didn't understand me," cried Cézanne.
"He never understood me." And it was this thought
which almost killed the man. Cézanne could excuse the
use of himself as model, could overlook unkind exaggerations of physical and mental peculiarities presented to
the whole world of novel readers. What he could not
forgive was the insincerity of Zola's attitude to him over
the years. He had put all his trust in Zola. After thirty-
four years this trust was publicly thrown back at him.

2

His reaction was immediate and typical. From the age of thirteen his life had been poised between the antagonistic influences of his father and Zola. Zola had opposed his father, had influenced son against father. The son had allowed himself to be influenced.

Hurriedly he attempted to make retribution. He cut Zola out of his life. He decided never to write, never to speak to him again. And he went straight over to Aix and told his father that he had been living with Hortense for seventeen years and had a son aged fourteen.

The disclosure was seventeen years too late. Old M. Cézanne received the news without surprise, without pleasure too. He had been hurt, and a rebound from wounded pride did not assuage the hurt. He said simply that as he did not expect to live long he would like his son to be married at once.

On April 28 Cézanne and Hortense were married in the registry office in the presence of the old couple. The following day they went through a church ceremony in Aix.

Six months later Louis-Auguste died. He was eighty-eight. Cézanne at forty-seven became a rich man. His share of the estate was not far short of half a million francs. Of this he gave one third to Hortense, put one third in trust for his son and kept the remaining third for himself.

CHAPTER SEVENTEEN

Painter Succeeds Man

1886–1895

ÉZANNE was to live another twenty years but most
that was loving in the man died in 1886. Zola's
act was a calamity. Misunderstood throughout his
first forty-seven years, Cézanne had clung ever closer to
the one man who professed to understand him. Belief in
his friend's affection and knowledge of the true Cézanne
kept him from absolute misanthropy. No need to see
Zola; to think of his faith was strength enough. Again and
again thought of Zola had stifled the pangs of conscience
when his father looked at him or tried to get into his
mind.

Then all was gone; his father was dead, uncomprehending to the last; and a few pages of type in a book had
destroyed three-quarters of a lifetime of illusion. Cézanne
found himself alone. The love he was still offered appeared valueless; his mother and Marie did not understand him, his son was too young, was in any case the
child of Hortense. Only the boy escaped the savage
reaction of the wounded man. For him Cézanne retained
a pathetic admiration which was to become almost absolute trust; almost, because he could never again trust
anyone completely; pathetic, because the boy was to grow

into the living image of Louis-Auguste and to regard his
father with much the same eyes as his grandfather.

For the rest, no one escaped censure. Cézanne could
not be said to withdraw from the world because he
had virtually withdrawn years earlier, but he became
violently antisocial. Suspicion, latent in him all his life,
was allowed full rein; it poisoned every relationship.
With every year his detestation of his fellow men seemed
to grow, and his efforts to appear even passably civil
dwindled to next to nothing. He criticized everything and
almost everybody; only his son and his father escaped
that scathing tongue; of them he said nothing but good.

Even Hortense did not escape the revulsion from
human beings. Her faults were two. She loved Paris and
the north better than Aix and the south, and refused
to live permanently in the latter. More serious still, she
had offended the puritan in her husband; by sexual attraction she had made him fling restraint away. The
puritan does not die, does not forget, cannot forgive
this one monstrous sin. There was no open break, no
official separation, but a gradual falling away. For a
few years she continued to pose for him, but she spent
more and more time in Paris, less and less time in Aix.
He lived with his mother and Marie at the Jas de Bouffan.
After a prolonged stay with Hortense and the boy in
Switzerland in 1890 the relationship disintegrated further.
His insistence soon afterward that they return to Aix to
live completed the breach. The forms were observed occasionally but all feeling was gone. Cézanne even criticized her openly to passing acquaintances.

2

To trace the history of the man in detail during the
nine years after the publication of *L'Œuvre* would be

painful and unprofitable. He had become truly a shadow of himself, but an only too substantial shadow with unpleasant characteristics monstrously elongated. He provided local gossip with a wealth of material in these years of anarchic existence; the people of Aix made the most of it. He was the chief architect of the legend of Cézanne the Impossible, which has lived to the present day.

The history of the painter is another matter. In the lives of many artists failure in personal relationships turns into a source of creative power. This was particularly true of Cézanne. The virtual death of the man as a social being gave the painter his chance, a chance which he took with both hands. The revelation of his one friend's ignorance and disloyalty followed by the death of an unappeased, disappointed father confirmed Cézanne in his antisocial attitude; at forty-seven he came back with a rush of angry hurt to the defensive, wary life of early schooldays; he had been right after all. But compensation is one of the laws of life. For Cézanne to lose hope of getting on terms with people was simply to shift this longing for communication firmly and finally to the painter, who was to struggle for the rest of his life to get on terms with nature. He had come much of the way before the disaster; he now gave himself body and soul to the quest; rarely before and never since has there been such inexorable, self-denying devotion to art.

Nor was the emergence of the true Cézanne simply a question of turning his whole heart into his work. His virtual rejection of human relationships—or, to look at it another way, his admission of failure in life—altered his attitude toward painting. How a happy, contented, self-expressed Cézanne would have painted can never be known; the work the world admires today was formed in the fire of suffering and loneliness. The "sensation" he had been seeking for so many years was finally captured only at this cost; he could have discovered it in no other way.

The change is seen fairly soon, as soon as he could pull himself together after the shock. There were to be no more attempts at the Salon, the reason for them having disappeared. Instead came a prolonged, determined attempt at the discovery and perfection of his individual vision as painter. The vague feelings he had had in L'Estaque in 1882 when studying the geometrical patterns of the houses came back to him as a strong conviction. He could not be an Impressionist. To him, shocked away from pure and obvious passion, the Impressionists' work appeared as emotional painting first and foremost, the surface emotion of delight in light and color seen at one particular moment by one particular eye. The intellect, he now believed, must impose form and give depth to a painting by analyzing the *motif* before a brush touched canvas. "The painter," he explained, "possesses two things, an eye and a brain. The two must work together. Both must be developed. But developed to meet the needs of the painter: the eye by looking at nature, the brain by logically organizing the sensations which lead to the form of expression."

Here was revolution which would have shocked the Guerbois gatherings. He explains each function clearly again and again during these later years of his life. For instance, he tells the youthful admirer of Gauguin, Émile Bernard, who had turned to him: "Reproduce nature by the cylinder, the sphere, the cone, all placed in perspective so that each side of an object or plane is directed toward a central point. Lines parallel to the horizon give breadth, a section of nature, that's to say, or, if you prefer it, the spectacle spread before our eyes by the omnipotent Father and eternal God. Lines perpendicular to this horizon give depth. Now for us men nature is more depth than surface so we must introduce into our light vibrations, represented by reds and yellows, enough blue-ishness to convey the feeling of air."

Again, and to the same man, he says: "To make progress nature only can suffice. The eye trains itself by contact with her. It becomes concentric by sheer looking and working. That is to say, in an orange, a pear, a ball, a head there is a culminating point; and despite the terrific effect of light and shade and sensations of color, this point is always nearest to our eye; the edges of the objects retire to a central spot on our horizon."

These notes to a painter wishing to grasp the secret of Cézanne's "sensation" show how he had at last profited fully from the lesson of Pontoise. For years the full value of those many months of painting under Pissarro had stopped short at the north. Pissarro's admonitions and the lack of obvious charm in northern motifs had joined to teach Cézanne discipline, had taught him to search for hidden tone values, hidden color effects. But the countryside of the north was never congenial to him. This was an intellectual exercise. The countryside of the Midi excited him; his passions roused by it, he was a flame of emotion at the easel; the discipline learned by the side of Pissarro was muted 500 miles to the south. Then came the blow, hurtful but healthy too, of L'Œuvre. His consequent reaction to human relationships imposed a new discipline, the discipline of the passionate man thwarted into clear thinking. This intellectual attitude of the painter linked instinctively with memories of Pissarro's reiterations. Cézanne began to study the southern scene with the mental application he had given years earlier to the work at Pontoise and Auvers; he strove to see what lay behind the gaudy appearance, analyzed the forms.

So he is found exclaiming, "Here, on the river bank, the motifs multiply. The same subject seen from a different angle provides a study of the greatest interest, and so varied that I could occupy myself for months without moving my position, but just leaning sometimes to the right, sometimes to the left."

This little scene of Cézanne at work was, as it happens, written to his son in the last year of his life. But it holds good for any of his last twenty years: from start to finish he was the tireless searcher, keen mind and hot blood victoriously allied.

3 ⤴

For nine years he struggled to obtain recognition as an important painter, and with two exceptions struggled in vain. These were years of movement. It is a commonplace that the creator feels a special need for repeated change of scene; the mere listing of the addresses of Beethoven, Chopin, Tchaikovsky, for instance, is dizzying. Nor is this agitated existence confined to composers; poets, novelists, painters often display a similar and understandable restlessness.

Up to the break with Zola, Cézanne had had what in comparison with most painters was a static existence; the call of the south had been a constant stabilizing influence. But in the nine years from 1886, even the beloved southern scene and climate could not hold him for more than a few months at a time.

The major reason for this restlessness was of course the shock of losing Zola. Cézanne acted like a man bereaved, as he was, and left solitary. His mother and Marie had long since ceased to mean more to him than the surroundings of the Jas de Bouffan in which all three lived;

to a man of his passionate temperament the puerilities of
the aging Mme Cézanne and the rigid Catholicism with
which the spinster Marie consoled herself were alike incapable of giving him relief. Even when he followed his
sister into the Catholic faith he fell foul of the priests,
questioned everything, and remained largely unsatisfied.
The affection he lavished, secretly for the most part, on his
son was not returned in equal measure. As he grew up,
young Paul, though affectionate, respectful, and helpful,
made quite clear that he stood by his mother, literally and
in sympathy.

There was, in short, no substitute for his old school
friend. His heart had been given to Zola for more than
half a lifetime; Zola had become a habit and a necessity.
So, bereft of Zola at a blow, he roamed about uncharac-
teristically, seeking solace in work and new surroundings.

But there was a second reason for these years of movement: his sense of the passage of time. Before the period
ended he was in his middle fifties, unwell—he developed
diabetes—and convinced that he had not many years to
live. Yet he remained unknown; the scandal of his canvases
at the Impressionist exhibitions had long since been forgotten, and his correspondence with every man of moment, Chocquet partially excepted, had died away. In
Parisian art circles he was rarely mentioned; a generation
of painters and art critics was growing up which had never
heard the name of Cézanne or had heard it only in the
form of stupid gossip, stories of the wild hermit of Aix.

This death in life was agony to one who believed himself on the one hand to be painting better than ever and
on the other less than ever able to mix with his fellow men.
The one virtually canceled the other; the chances of his
work being noticed, let alone acclaimed, were pitifully
slender.

So he roamed, easel and canvases on back, living with a frugality which would have been astonishing in a rich man who was not a Cézanne, and in a state of disorder, not to say filth, which would have told anybody with insight how greatly he suffered.

By 1888 he was back in Paris where, as if to plumb the full depth of wretchedness, he took the studio he had occupied next to Guillaumin in 1875, the studio Claude Lantier was portrayed in by Zola. He did not, because he could not, stay there long; leaving it as a base, he painted in the outskirts of Paris, mainly around Chantilly and in the Fontainebleau forest.

In Paris he met only Guillaumin and, once or twice, the still enthusiastic Chocquet, whose wish to push him was frustrated time and again almost as much by Cézanne's lack of assurance as by his lack of reputation. "Chance," he told Chocquet wistfully, "has not favored me with a self-confidence equals to yours," and he praised without envy the "splendid balance of the essential faculties" in Chocquet and his wife. But the generous man was determined on some sort of gesture; he regarded Cézanne in the wilderness as a tragedy for French painting as much as for the man. In 1889 his chance came. It was the year of the Exposition Universelle. As usual there was an exhibition of French painting, all of it academic but for a canvas or two by Pissarro and Monet. Chocquet was asked by the organizers to lend or persuade a friend to lend (the truth is not clear) an *objet d' art* for the term of the Fair. He did so but with a stipulation, that they include a picture by Cézanne. So Cézanne found himself after years of exile once again mentioned in a catalogue of an exhibition. And that was about all he did find. There was no chance that a canvas of his (in this case *La Maison du Pendu*, already shown in the first Impressionist exhibition)

would be allowed to be seen. The organizers were forced
to show it, but by hanging it high and away from the light
they rendered it practically invisible.

Cézanne no doubt stared up at it more than once—he
was still working on and off at Rue d'Anjou—but he was
alone in noticing it; not a word was said in the many press
reviews of the show.

Perhaps in an attempt to soothe his hurt feelings Chocquet carried him off, after heaven knows what efforts
at persuasion, to his summer house in Normandy. There
Cézanne made another fine portrait of his host before,
scared away by the Chocquets' elegance of living, he retired suddenly to Aix.

That autumn Renoir joined him; there had been vague
talk of a *quid pro quo* for the stay at La Roche-Guyon—
a stay better forgotten by all—and at last the arrangement
was made; Renoir rented the summer house of Rose's
husband near Aix.

The experiment was little more successful than Cézanne's sojourn at La Roche. The two men painted together
in the country round Aix, but something disturbed their
relationship. The something is said to have been Cézanne's fits of ill humor. This excuse has too often been
regarded as all-explanatory in Cézanne's later years. He
was touchy, suspicious, unable to trust another man's affection or admiration, but never without initial cause. He
and Renoir agreed on one subject, the treatment of the
nude; Cézanne's many studies of bathers make this only
too clear. For the rest the likelihood of agreement was
scanty. Cézanne was incapable of sentimentalism, of the
merely pretty-pretty. Renoir was not. It is unnecessary to
look further for disagreement and, given this, Cézanne's
utterly frank and disconcerting expression of it.

They parted abruptly, never to meet again in intimacy,

but—a significant fact—with the younger man's respect
for Cézanne's work unimpaired.

4 ~~~~

Toward the end of this year, 1889, Cézanne received
an unexpected compliment—unexpected by him, that is.
He was invited by Les XX of Brussels to exhibit there
the following year. This group of avant-garde Belgian
painters had for the previous five years invited advanced
foreign artists to show their work. Monet, Pissarro, Gau-
gain, and Guillaumin had already exhibited, and the invitation to Cézanne followed favorable comments on his
paintings by one or all of them to the organizer, Octave
Maus. Other painters invited to exhibit in 1890 were Sisley
and Van Gogh.

Cézanne accepted the invitation gladly. His letter doing so was a document of which any man might be proud.
For Maus had prefaced his invitation with a comment
showing clearly that he believed the long-standing story
of an impossibly vain Cézanne refusing through pique to
join the Impressionists. In reply Cézanne disdained the
motive gossip had foisted on him and set down firmly but
humbly his reason for seeking obscurity: "I made up my
mind to work in silence until the day when I felt myself
capable of defending my attempts in theory as well as
in practice."

This, one of the noblest affirmations made by an artist
in the history of man, did not then and has not since received the notice it deserves. And this, so shortsighted
is the world, partly because it is couched in crude, un-
rhetorical, not to say ungrammatical language. Yet had
Cézanne chosen to make his presence felt in Paris he would
years earlier have become one of the city's most notable

men. His uncouthness and blunt speech would have done nothing to prevent this fame; Paris has always adored the eccentric. But he who dearly wanted fame and had yearned for it since his youth would not take it on any terms but the one. He chose the wilderness because he believed that the notice he would win in Paris would be won falsely.

He could not resist the offer from Brussels, but in the event he could have resisted it without loss. The 1890 exhibition of Les XX was overlaid by the happenings at its *vernissage* dinner, when the Belgian painter Henry de Groux's offensive remarks on the work of Van Gogh were ended by a challenge from Toulouse-Lautrec. After this excitement over a duel which never took place, the actual show won little attention. Cézanne's exhibits, including *La Maison du Pendu, Étude de Paysage, Une Chaumière à Auvers-sur-Oise* and a sketch of bathers, were, Mme Maus afterward said, "scarcely noticed." They were, of course, early works, Cézanne still hugging to himself the many experiments expressing his "sensation." Not that he grudged the world a sight of them; he remained through this period to 1895 dissatisfied with work all of which has long since been adjudged of the highest order.

The result of the exhibition, or the lack of it, drove him afield once more. This time he made a radical departure, spending the five spring and summer months in Switzerland with his wife and son. This solitary period which Cézanne was to spend outside France was not a success. Rumor has it, probably with greater accuracy than usual, that Hortense persuaded him to the trip; his caustic remarks on her fondness for the delicacies of Swiss pastry cooks certainly suggests it. Hortense's life since the break with Zola had not been a happy one; she had dwindled to the role she first occupied in Cézanne's life, of the one model who could be relied on not to move a muscle for hours at a time. She posed again and again, her son too, but without enthusiasm. A not unattractive woman in her early forties cannot easily be brought to consider this her only use. Hortense became restive.

The holiday in Switzerland may have pleased her and her son; it did not please Cézanne. They traveled widely and spent much money. He had never been enthusiastic about the spending of money; now that he had more than he could do with, he suffered visibly and audibly if he did not get his money's worth. He signed himself once as Père Goriot; in fun and serious too, ironic with himself as with everyone else. His money's worth was obtainable only in work. And unhappily the dramatic landscape of Switzerland did not move the painter; he could settle to nothing; he painted nothing of value.

Back he went to Aix in autumn, furious at the loss of precious time. At the Jas de Bouffan he began one of his most famous series of paintings, the card players of the local auberge.

But he could not rest even in this loved spot. For the next three years until autumn 1894, he roamed up and down France; Aix to Paris, Paris to Fontainebleau, Fontainebleau to Aix, up again to paint by the Seine, the Marne, the Oise, pulled irresistibly back to Aix only to leave again after a month or two of wandering between Gardanne and L'Estaque for Fontainebleau, Chantilly or wherever the mood took him.

5 ⟶

Three years: years of nothingness, years of fulfillment too. Wherever he went, his canvases, brushes, and colors went, too. He worked grimly, with infinite patience, a lonely, silent man who looked like a tramp and thought like a god.

In the autumn of 1894 this curious combination of restlessness in movement and dogged perseverance in work was arrested unexpectedly by a stay at the inn at Giverny. Cézanne and Monet, never intimate, had seen little of each other since the Guerbois days. But except for the period when Monet and Pissarro differed about the future of the Impressionist exhibitions and Cézanne loyally supported Pissarro, Cézanne had always respected Monet and his work. The saying "Monet is only an eye, but what an eye!" has been variously attributed to Cézanne and Degas. It has the mark of Degas. But if Cézanne did not say it, he thought it and more. Monet's life had been dedicated to painting. He had suffered for it physically, mentally, emotionally. His wife had died for lack of food. He had been snubbed, despised, rejected year after year. But he had never given up, never even wavered. And he never ceased to experiment. All this won Cézanne's admiration. Personally, Monet was a blunt, hearty Norman without affectation, a man to whom Cézanne could talk without fear of criticism. They did not in fact talk much because they met seldom. But each watched the other's progress. Cézanne was soon to describe Monet's Rouen cathedral series as "the work of a well-balanced but impulsive artist who has captured to a greater degree than any other painter the intangible nuances of effects." More definitely, he was to declare after the death of Pissarro, "I despise all living painters except Monet and Renoir."

But the best proof of Cézanne's high regard for Monet is this surprising visit to Giverny on the Seine west of Paris where the younger painter had settled for life. Since the break with Zola eight years earlier Cézanne had isolated himself from all painters, all companions. Except for the few days with Chocquet, days guaranteed to frighten him off another experiment, he had been careful never to place himself within reach of anyone he knew, not even Pissarro. Now he took the plunge again and subjected himself daily, walking across from the inn, to the perils of another man's house. Life at Giverny differed greatly from life at Médan; it was simple and sincere, almost monastic; but at Giverny were guests, invited deliberately to meet the almost fabulous recluse of Aix; and guests, to Cézanne, spelled embarrassment, annoyance; they were the incarnation of frivolity and antiwork.

For a time he survived the ordeal with comparative calm. His greatest trial was the young Georges Clemenceau, who loved to twist the lion's tail. Clemenceau mischievously fastened on the religious beliefs of the painter; skeptic himself and a brilliant debater, he reduced the taciturn Catholic to an incoherently mumbling mass of helpless fury. Clemenceau would hastily redeem himself by stories and jokes so witty that even an angered Cézanne laughed himself into appeasement. However, his considered and wary opinion was: "For a man like me who can't master ordinary life, it is safer to rest on Rome."

He was described at Monet's by another visitor, the middle-aged daughter of an American banker, Mary Cassatt, who, influenced by Degas, had thrown in her lot with the Impressionists in the years after Cézanne's withdrawal. She was talented, amiable, but not very perceptive, quoting Daudet to describe the man from the Midi: "When I first saw him I thought he looked like a cutthroat with large red eyeballs standing out from his head in a most ferocious manner, a rather fierce-looking pointed beard, quite gray, and an excited way of talking that positively made the dishes rattle."

She was equally startled by his table manners, or lack

of them: scraping of soup plate, taking chop in fingers, eating and gesturing with his only implement, the knife.

This vision of Cézanne punctiliously acting out the peasant, defense mechanism hard at work, was contradicted to the confusion of the naïve guest; for she found him polite, deferential to the "stupid" maid, and always quick to pull off the old tam-o'shanter, worn to protect his bald head, when he entered a room.

Cézanne had, Mary Cassatt noted, become rather less the wild man than formerly; the great bushy beard had disappeared forever, in its place gray-white mustaches and a beard more or less neatly clipped to a point.

Rodin was there, and Octave Mirbeau, but of all the guests Gustave Geffroy proved most congenial. This young and promising critic was impressed from the moment he persuaded Cézanne to show him the canvases spread higgledy-piggledy about the room at the inn along the road. His admiration was too obvious for doubt even from the cautious painter. Cézanne relaxed, was heard to laugh, actually attempted what in another man would be called repartee. In gratitude he meditated a portrait of Geffroy, but was too diffident to suggest it.

As for his host, bluff, honest, and as devoted to his work as even Cézanne could wish, the southerner was to express his feelings very typically in language and in time; nearly a year was to pass before he could bring himself to the point. "May I tell you," he wrote at last, "how glad I was of the moral support I met beside you and which has given such stimulation to my painting?"

The support was deliberate, had he but known. Cézanne, Monet told a friend, was "a true artist too much tormented by self-doubts. He needs a helping hand." Some of Monet's helping hands were successful—the unpretentious talks about painting problems, for example—but before very long he ran foul of something in Cézanne which was past reckoning. The legacy of distrust from the Zola affair was always liable to influence a modesty and a sensibility so extreme as to be practically unimaginable by the normal man. Monet with genuine kindness and respect arranged an informal dinner to Cézanne, inviting Renoir and Sisley for the purpose. He said nothing to Cézanne until the meal was about to begin. Then: "Here we are, all together and happy to have the chance of telling you how fond of you we are and how much we admire your work."

At this Cézanne's head fell and his eyes filled with tears. "Ah, Monet, even you make fun of me!" he murmured, and before anyone could speak he was up and making for the door. No protestations could move him; there and then he left the room, house, and village. He walked straight off without troubling or remembering to collect his canvases, and was never seen at Giverny again. The next day Monet packed up his canvases and sent them to Aix after him.

"I am back in the south which perhaps I ought never to have left." This to Monet the following summer could have served for the autumn of 1894; that was how the stricken man felt. Actually, the remark referred to the Geffroy portrait. For after much hesitation Cézanne, moved to action by an article Geffroy had written on his painting, went so far as to announce, when he returned to Paris, that he meditated calling on the author "to say how do you do and to put before you a plan I have been alternately considering and rejecting."

This was in the spring of 1895. The visit somehow got itself paid, the project discussed, and Geffroy agreed gladly to sit for his portrait.

Three months later Cézanne rushed back to Aix with

the remark to Monet already quoted and an "I am rather embarrassed by the poor results I've obtained after so many sittings."

That was the truth, yet not the whole truth. This came out years later, in an expansive moment. "He talked too much of Clemenceau," explained Cézanne. He meant, simply, "He talked." The portrait, never finished, was a superb piece of work.

6 ～

Geffroy could write of Cézanne as "the precursor" of Impressionism; Monet, Renoir, Pissarro could praise him to their friends; the young painters who frequented Tanguy's shop could speak reverently of the few extraordinary canvases there. All this and more was powerless to arouse general interest.

Geffroy tried to whip up curiosity about this legendary figure: "a man at once famous and unknown, rarely in contact with the public but influencing the restless seekers in painting; known only to the few, living in wild isolation, reappearing then disappearing. . . . All the scanty facts about his life, the work produced in secret, the rare canvases which seem to follow none of the accepted rules . . . give him a strange kind of renown."

The effort did not succeed. Cézanne's "renown" was more journalism than fact. No words could alter the bald truth that the art lovers of Paris had not seen his work publicly displayed since 1877, nearly twenty years earlier. Without display a painter cannot make himself known. The one passable substitute for regular exhibitions of paintings, exhibitions of the man, was even scarcer; though often enough in Paris and the surrounding country Cézanne had for years taken extravagant precautions to avoid even the most casual of encounters. One incident will serve for all. One day on the quay he saw Sisley and Guillaumin bearing down on him. Before they could reach him he had made urgent and unmistakable signs to them; he wished them not to acknowledge him. Mystified, hurt but obedient, they crossed the street and passed in silence.

This kind of behavior led to gossip but not to fame. The true word about the standing of "this fantastic figure" was spoken by the critic Mellerio: "Cézanne," he said, "although still living is spoken of as though he were dead."

The prices of his canvases, on the rare occasions when they came before the public eye, bore out this death-in-life reputation. In 1893 Caillebotte died and, in accordance with the terms of the will made when he first adopted the Impressionists years earlier, his collection was left to the Luxembourg. After a long and undignified squabble, the academicians fighting to prevent "this heap of excrement," the work of "anarchists and madmen," from being hung in a state museum, some two-thirds of the collection was accepted. As is customary, the accepted pictures were given an approximate price. The Cézannes were valued at 750 francs, less than half that of any other Impressionist, less than a sixth of the Manet, Monet, and Renoir canvases.

This decisive confirmation of the art world's neglect of Cézanne was strengthened the very next year, in 1894, when another death, that of Tanguy, threw six Cézanne canvases on to the market. At the auction of Tanguy's effects the Cézannes fetched the pitiful sums of from 45 to 215 francs each.

As a painter, then, Cézanne remained either not known or, when known, not appreciated. Not until the end of

1895, when he was within a few weeks of his fifty-seventh birthday, did this nationwide neglect show its first sign of change, a change that was to lead to his elevation as the greatest of the Post-Impressionists and perhaps the greatest of all nineteenth-century painters.

This dramatic change from utter negation to the beginnings of world fame was set in motion at 39 Rue Laffitte, the shop of Ambroise Vollard.

CHAPTER EIGHTEEN

Mortal Victory

1895–1906

THE last eleven years of Cézanne's life are in almost every way an improvement on the previous nine. They began with the first success his work had ever won, and despite illness, discouragement, malicious gossip, and personal sorrow, the impetus given by this success never wholly died away. Threatened it often was, but the painter, once encouraged, refused to be disheartened. These eleven years, for all their melancholy moments, are in essence years of triumphant progress, every adversity being brushed aside or beaten down. The record of the closing years of an elderly man is seldom inspiring, but Cézanne's tenacity of purpose and faith in his destiny provide an exhilarating exception. Even the man, apparently crushed into misanthropy, rose from time to time on the wings of the painter.

He had to thank Pissarro for this abrupt lift into prominence. In January, 1894, the minor French painter John Lewis Brown introduced Pissarro to Ambroise Vollard, then the newest thing in art dealers. A young and smart creole, Vollard was in many ways an impossible person, cheap, untrustworthy, flamboyant, and no friend to the truth. But he mingled with ambition a certain moral

courage and an eye for the painting of the future. Poor
Pissarro, like so many painters, could not afford to be
too particular; if Vollard would buy or could sell his
work, then the art dealer's morals or lack of them had to
be overlooked.

What Vollard really thought of the paintings he pushed
will never be known; he was intelligent enough to
realize that a reputation as purveyor of avant-garde
painters could lead to fame and fortune. It could also
lead to the bankruptcy court, and his distinction is that
he picked the right painters at the right time. This
flair served him in good stead. By the time Pissarro met
him he had bought Émile Bernard's collection of Gauguin, then in Tahiti. Bernard let them go cheaply, declaring that he had taught Gauguin all the essentials
of the Post-Impressionist technique and aim, and that in
any case he could, if he chose, do them better himself.
Vollard thought differently but kept his own counsel
until the canvases were handed over. Then he began his
propaganda; well-timed, for Gauguin was just then coming into fashion with one or two of the wealthy collectors.

Pissarro, who had been flirting with the pointillism of
Seurat, interested Vollard, too, but mildly, for Pissarro,
even the pointillist, was no longer news. What he wanted
was precisely what Pissarro now offered him. For Pissarro, regarding Cézanne as his own creation going to
waste in the desert, made haste, his own sales settled,
to show Vollard the canvases Cézanne had given him
years ago in return for his hospitality.

Vollard's eyes sparkled when he saw them. There, he
realized immediately, was the sensation he was after;
a forgotten painter whom he, Vollard, would bring to
life. A great one, too, the equal of Gauguin, already
marked down as his property. Cézanne secured, and he

would have in his hands the two master painters of the future.

How much was sensationalism, how much divination in all this is of little moment. Vollard found Cézanne a tough nut to crack; unlike Gauguin, who was soon to turn over to him his whole output, he was not in need of money. Not for twenty-two months, in November, 1895, did Vollard collect enough paintings to open the first one-man show of Cézanne ever held.

Vollard's timing was excellent. The Impressionists had done their work. In the twenty years since their first exhibition, years spent by Cézanne mostly out of sight, the public had grown accustomed to what it had shrieked at and abused; Monet, chief of the Impressionists, had become widely honored and admired; all had ardent followers. Art lovers and purchasers were almost ready for the next stage. Already Gauguin's work was selling. Now came Cézanne. And this time there was no laughter, no hysterics, no vulgar cartoons. Opposition there was, for the Colonel Blimps live long. The usual reference to "atrocities" appeared in one journal, and in another, Le Temps, a friend of Zola significantly spoke of the "unfulfilled" Cézanne who remained "incapable of judging himself."

But adverse reports were the exceptions. Respect even when uncomprehending was the general rule. There was positive enthusiasm, too. "The new master of still life," declared Thadée Natanson. "One of the finest, greatest personalities of our time," wrote Geffroy, "supremely sincere, intense and artless, rugged and subtle. His work will be hung in the Louvre." And Arsène Alexandre, under the heading "Claude Lantier," in Le Figaro made tardy reparation for years of silence. "When L'Œuvre, that romantic epic of painting, appeared," he said, ". . .

some fairly well-informed critics wrote that Claude
Lantier, the main character in the novel, the wretched
neurotic painter who finally hangs himself before his
picture, was a portrait of Cézanne. This was all that was
needed for people interested in gossip and unprintable
tit-bits about the life of artists to spread the weirdest
tales about a painter who could do nothing to contradict
them and probably would not if he could. . . . Today
Zola's friend, the mysterious man from Provence, the
painter at once incomplete and inventive, shy and un-
civilized, has suddenly been discovered to be a great
man."

The painters were enthusiastic, and none more than the
old Pissarro, who saw his faith and teaching and encouragement at long last rewarded. Cut off from Cézanne
for years, an occasional word at the rare gallery-meeting
their only contact, he had lost touch with his work.
When he saw what Cézanne had done with his lost
years, he was staggered. He wrote here, there, and everywhere, volubly excited. "At Vollard's there is a very complete exhibition of Cézanne's works. Still lives of astonishing perfection and some unfinished works really outstanding for their character and savagery. . . . I don't
expect they'll be understood."

This seeming quite inadequate, he tried again: ". . . ex-
quisite things, *still lives*, of irreproachable finish, *others
very much worked on* of yet greater beauty even though
left uncompleted, *landscapes, nudes,* and *heads* unfinished
yet grand, so painted, so molded. Why? Sensation is
there!"

While Pissarro was standing before the pictures "admiring this strange, disconcerting impression of Cézanne,"
Renoir came into Vollard's shop. "My enthusiasm paled
before his. Degas himself is seduced by the charm of

this subtle savage, Monet, all of us. . . . As Renoir said so well, these paintings have the indefinable quality of the things at Pompeii, so unpolished yet so admirable."

The old painter came again and again, embroiled from time to time in discussions about the genesis of the work in question. He had to endure many shocks from which he reacted indignantly, beard waving, eyes flashing. "Heymann had the cheek to repeat the absurdity that Cézanne was influenced by Guillaumin!" Again: "This ignorant fool claims that Cézanne was for a time under the influence of *Monet*. This is the limit eh? However, Gauguin knows all about the Cézanne studies done in Auvers, Pontoise, and elsewhere."

Then came the flat statement that Cézanne had developed his own style uninfluenced by anyone. That, declared Pissarro, was also rubbish: Cézanne had been influenced by Delacroix, Courbet, Manet, "and by me at Pontoise and I by him. In Cézanne's show at Vollard's there are certain landscapes of Auvers and Pontoise similar to mine. Ye gods! Naturally! We were always together." But at this moment the greatness of Pissarro rose above vanity: "But this is certain, each of us kept the one thing that matters, his own 'sensation.' "

These assertions, denials, claims, counter-claims, were themselves a sign that the painter had at last thrust himself into general notice. Who had bothered before the Vollard show to discuss derivations, influences, or anything else in connection with Cézanne? This aspect of the matter was clear to Pissarro. "Degas and Renoir are enthusiastic about Cézanne's work. Vollard showed me a drawing of fruit which they both wanted; they drew lots." Yet even this admiration passed the bounds he would have expected; he let out a cry of incredulous triumph: "Degas passionately attached to Cézanne's sketches—what do you think of that!" He could not believe that such advanced work would win favor from the experts, let alone the public. "You would hardly credit," he told his son, "how difficult I find it to make certain collectors appreciate the extraordinary great qualities of Cézanne. I suppose centuries will pass before they are understood."

In this Pissarro was mistaken. Like the gentler Chocquet (recently dead) before him, he underestimated instinctive reaction to his own bludgeoning tactics; the collectors wanted to make up their own minds, not to be shouted into them. True enough, Cézanne was to remain intrinsically the painters' painter, the model for thousands of ambitious and enthusiastic young men. Nevertheless, within half a century of Pissarro's forecasts his paintings were to be found, treasured, in galleries and homes throughout the world.

2

The subdued noise of the exhibition reached Cézanne but did not stir him. The thought that for the first time in thirty years of painting he had been treated almost without obloquy or as the big joke of Paris was sobering rather than encouraging. His chief feeling was bitterness. He felt old, tired, incapable of joy. Crippled by self-doubt since his birth, scorned and ridiculed by most of his fellow painters and all his public, betrayed by his best friend, how could he believe that the tide had turned? At fifty-seven he remained at heart the youth of seventeen mooching along the streets not daring to lift his head when one of the belles of Aix passed, for fear that she would shame him by a public cut. The belle had become fame, that was the whole difference in forty years; Cézanne's attitude had not changed.

For a long time he would not or dared not see that his genius was at last being acknowledged. He had never lost faith in his potential greatness as painter but had begun to fear that the potentiality was all. Zola's obvious reservations, giving a fearful significance to his father's skeptical smile and intensifying his own chronic lack of self-confidence, had started the rot. Nothing which had happened since was of a nature to console or strengthen him.

So his first response to the Vollard show was a complaint weeks after all was over: why could the critics not leave him in peace? He wanted simply to work in obscurity.

Only Cézanne could react thus and remain sincere. The doubts of a lifetime were not to be chased away by one exhibition and a few favorable remarks. The caution of the peasant and the unreasoning protective impulse of the wounded joined to erect this camouflage of unbelief.

But no amount of skepticism could resist forever the evidence that followed. The process was slow and still continuing when Cézanne died. It is most improbable that he would have been greatly affected even by some dramatic stroke of fortune, but he was not put to the test. His reward was as he would have preferred it, a quiet and almost unnoticeable increase of regard for his work.

Vollard was the obvious, if not the only influence behind this gradual change in the taste of the art-concious people of Paris. The stir caused by his exhibition, added possibly to a genuine admiration—with such a man as Vollard there is no certainty—had developed in him a kind of single-minded passion. By the next year, 1869, Pissarro was reporting ruefully of a visit to the dealer's shop: "I went to show him three things. He didn't even look at them; he left me stranded there to show me a Cézanne."

By the next year, 1897, Vollard had set out to make a corner in Cézannes. He bought every painting he could discover. He went to Fontainebleau, where Cézanne was working, and bought the complete collection in the studio. He went down to Aix and routed out the canvases Cézanne had given away and thrown away, too. He was to tell many amusing stories about this search for Cézannes. Tall stories too; one and all are to a greater or lesser degree apocryphal. The single undoubted truth is that the owners of these canvases in Aix and district had almost to a man relegated them to attics, barns, outhouses. To own a Cézanne in Aix was no honor.

The result of this intensive drive was slow but sure as Vollard established his own reputation in Paris. Two years later, in 1899, Chocquet's widow died and her Cézanne collection was sold. It averaged 1700 francs per picture (one of them, his favorite, *La Maison du Pendu,* fetching 6200 francs). Later that year, a Cézanne landscape fetched an even higher figure 6450 francs. The buyer was Monet. "They are beginning to catch on," the elated Vollard wrote to Gauguin.

Next year came the great Exposition Universelle with its famous Centenary Exhibition of French painting. Once more it is Pissarro who reports, astonished: "We . . . the Impressionists . . . have a room. . . . There will even be some Cézannes." Followed by: "And what's more, he is all the fashion. It is amazing!"

3 ⬸

There was another influence at work, and one which Cézanne welcomed practically without reservation. This was the admiration and example of the younger generation of painters. There was a time when Cézanne had longed for fame and had bitterly complained that he could not even earn a living from painting. But these wishes, the great and the small, had not been for his own sake. Now, his father dead, he cared about neither. He was preoccupied by what he called "the incessant pursuit of the one and only goal . . . to render—whatever our temperament or power in the presence of nature may be—the likeness of what we see, forgetting everything that has appeared before our day." This pursuit was for him neither selfish nor selfless, it was a duty. He was put on this earth with a gift, he had to develop that gift—that was his simple thought.

He was not given to self-analysis, all his powers in that direction being devoted to dissection of the motif so that he could render it truthfully in his own eyes. But once at least he expressed awareness of the logical end to his labors. "I am working doggedly," he wrote to Vollard. "I catch a glimpse of the Promised Land. Shall I be like the great leader of the Hebrews or shall I be permitted to enter?"

When Cézanne spoke he often regretted what he had said. When he wrote he meant every labored word of it. The analogy explains the man: Moses was leading his people to the promised land, Cézanne hoped to do so in his way. His greatest moments of happiness away from his work in these last years came to him when he realized that he had a following and that after his death his work would be carried on.

The history of this following began before Vollard, but took longer to manifest itself because the young painters were without power. For years Cézanne himself knew nothing of it. It began in the little shop in Rue Clauzel in Tanguy's final years. There the advanced young painters gathered, Maurice Denis, Émile Bernard, Seurat, Signac, and the older Vincent van Gogh and Gauguin. One of the young men, Bernard, has left an account of Tanguy producing his Cézannes for inspection. If allowance is made for a certain romanticism, the account rings true. "One went there," he says, "as to a museum, to see the few sketches by this unknown painter living in Aix who, displeased with his work and the world, used to destroy his paintings." When Tanguy was asked to show his Cézannes, he "disappeared into a dark room and reappeared a moment later carrying a medium-sized package carefully tied up, a mysterious smile on his thick lips, emotion shining in his moist eyes. He untied the string feverishly and, using the back of a chair as an easel, exhibited the paintings one after another in a religious silence."

Tanguy had, another visitor noticed, "a curious way of first looking down at his picture with all the fond love of a mother and then looking up at you over his glasses, as if begging you to admire his beloved children." He would wait whilst—this is Bernard again—"the visitors commented on them, pointing out details, enthusing over the color, subject matter, and style. When they had done, Tanguy talked about the painter. 'Papa Cézanne,' he would say, 'is never satisfied with what he does, he abandons it before he has finished. When he moves he makes a point of leaving his canvases behind; when he

paints out of doors he abandons them in the woods or
fields. He works very slowly, the least thing costs him
great effort, there is nothing accidental in his painting.' "

Tanguy, too, was inclined to romanticize the object of
admiration—he was a sentimental as well as lovable man
—but the admiration was so genuine that his hearers
swallowed everything and went away to embroider the
legend of the painter-recluse. It was a story to appeal to
the young and ardent avant-garde, this man of the Midi
fighting a lone battle against public prejudice and private
temperament.

Not all subscribed at once to the general view that the
canvases Tanguy propped on chairs were indubitable
great works of art pointing the way to the future. Argument waxed hot and tempers were lost. But when Gauguin
was there the discussions could have only one end. He
had, after all, painted with the master. One young man
disdainfully described the canvases as daubs. With a
bang of his decorated Breton stick on the floor, Gauguin
said in his loud, calm, authoritative voice, "Nothing
looks more like a daub than a masterpiece!"

Gauguin's masterful assurance that Cézanne was the
man to follow carried into his forward-looking group at
Pont-Aven with Bernard as youthful sub-lieutenant. It
was taken over by the rebellious Nabis of the École
Julian, Denis, Bonnard, Serusier, Vuillard, K. X. Roussel,
who had all, as Denis put it, "discovered with enormous
emotion the work of Paul Cézanne."

When Gauguin, too great to remain a disciple, cast his
own course and disappeared into Tahiti, the younger and
less gifted men gravitated toward Cézanne. Bernard wrote
admiringly to Aix, began to write publicly (though not
always accurately) about the neglected master. Denis,
with one eye on Gauguin and the other on Cézanne,

composed his afterward famous "*se rappeler qu'un tableau avant d'être un cheval de bataille, une femme nue ou une quelconque anecdote est essentiellement une surface plane recouverte de couleurs en un certain ordre assemblées.*" By 1901 his admiration had reached such a pitch that he painted and exhibited at the Salon his *Hommage à Cézanne*, the group of men who met to honor the man most of them had never seen.

Young painters followed these leads, wrote hopeful, worshipping letters, called on Cézanne, begged to be allowed to work with him. Invitations to exhibit in Paris, Brussels, Vienna, Berlin were received in Aix; no exhibition of advanced painters was considered complete without its Cézanne to mark the origin and the goal of every exhibitor.

In these years, the late nineties and the opening of the new century, Cézanne took the place in painting that Verlaine had occupied in poetry ten years earlier: little known by the public, regarded with doubt, envy, or disapproval by most of his contemporaries, revered by his juniors as the great adventurous genius of the age. The reaction of the two men could scarcely have been more different. Verlaine made himself the center of a crowd of young poets at the cafés of the Boulevard Saint-Michel, was hail-fellow-well-met with all, accepting free drinks, exchanging doubtful stories, and on occasion acting the great poet. He had practically stopped writing. Cézanne received his visitors kindly but did not make intimates of them; he was willing to help but made plain that his daily work came first; none must interfere with this primary reason for life. He was in his sixties and in pain; almost all his energies had to be conserved for the day in, day out visit to the *motif*. He had neither the time nor the patience for youthful exaggerations or puerilities, and his hot temper, rasped by physical suffering, flared up alarmingly when a guest praised the wrong man or the wrong painting. Nor would he accept flattery. He knew just how far he had gone on his chosen road; no young puppy could tell him that he was the great and perfect painter of France and expect to escape unscathed.

Not a sympathetic portrait. He was not loved by the young painters as Verlaine was loved by the young poets. But there was another side to the medal. Verlaine's insincerities, however great the charm with which they were uttered, drew many a hidden laugh. Cézanne was deeply respected by all, all the time, even in the moment of hurtful contact with his rough tongue. For Cézanne meant exactly what he said; his whole life shouted devotion to his conception of art. But a dedicated man is not the best of company. To a discerning eye, Cézanne could be infinitely appealing in his gruff, shy, modest, withdrawn way. He could also be terrifying. When asked a stupid question, above all when interrupted in his work, the dark eyes, reddened with age and the years of studying outdoor motifs, would flash ominously, the harsh voice shout insults.

In general he was too tired to do more than work. Advancing years and constant pain wearied him quickly. As he explained to one of his most persistent admirers: "After working all day trying to overcome the difficulties of reproducing nature, I feel the need of rest when evening comes and have no longer by that time sufficient mental elasticity for writing."

Cézanne had his own way of expressing gratification. It is perhaps unique. It is certainly, given the whole man, lovable. His reply to one fervent letter—and it can stand for all—was as follows. "You speak in your letter of my accomplishment in art. I believe that I am getting closer to it every day although with no little difficulty. If a strong feeling for nature—and most certainly I have that intensely—is the necessary starting point for the whole conception of art and determines the greatness and beauty of all future work, knowing how to express our feelings is not less essential and is only to be gained after very long experience. The approbation of others is a stimulant which it is sometimes wise to fight shy of. Feeling strong makes one modest."

He also summed up himself and his view of adulation briefly but competently in a letter to Vollard. Denis had reproached the master for refusing to exhibit in the Salon des Indépendants, the platform of the advanced young painters. Cézanne, who had already shown twice with them, gave way. He asked Vollard to send some of his work to Denis, asked with an apologetic, "It seems to me that it is difficult for me to detach myself from the young people who have shown themselves so sympathetic toward me." And to this honest though conventional remark the peasant-painter adds an inimitable, "And I don't think I shall jeopardize the progress of my work at all by exhibiting."

4 ⤳

The painter, then, marched on, his advance in general esteem being of a kind with his method of building up a picture, slow, methodical, sure. The man climbed with similar difficulty out of the pit into which he had fallen. He did not recover faith in humanity, he remained to the end a shadow of the man he could have been, but the years mellowed him. The years and other influences. There was the effect of the admiration of the young painters. There was the effect of an indomitable will fairly expressed at the age of sixty-seven in his "I am old and ill but I have sworn to myself to die painting rather than sink into the debasing dotage threatening all old men who allow themselves to be governed by passions which stupefy their senses." And there were two events which helped to release the man from his past.

The first of these events was the death of his mother. When old Mme Cézanne died in October, 1897, she was eighty-two. She had long been failing and was the cause of much trouble to Cézanne and his family. At her wish he brought Hortense and young Paul to live at the Jas de Bouffan in 1891; the boy, she thought, ought to be educated in Aix, and the place of her son and his wife was with her. Cézanne, peasant to the core, never questioned this wish: every peasant family in France lived in the house of the parents—why should he break the rule? But the result of it was general wretchedness. Both mother and sister resented the Parisienne Hortense, the unbeliever, the woman whom their Paul had married only to please his father. Both tried to undermine her influence with the young Paul. Yet, when not uniting against the unwanted, mother and daughter agreed in nothing: old Mme Cézanne had grown tedious and capricious with age, the spinster Marie had become the bitter religious bigot so familiar in the provinces of nineteenth-century France.

Hortense, disliking the south, longing for Paris, fearful for the future of her child, and furious with the women who kept her captive, showed her worst side to all. Cézanne did not escape; the result of this sudden passion for respectability provided a theme for her sharp tongue which she played with increasing virulence. As for Cézanne, who hated every domestic claim which got between him and his work, he went from one explosion of rage to another. The household broke into four hostile camps, Hortense and her son in one part of the house, Marie in another, Mme Cézanne in a third, and Cézanne storming about in his top-floor studio.

For six years this nightmare of a life went on. Cézanne became increasingly nervy and bad-tempered. His reputation in the town, never high, sank lower. He was the man who painted pictures scandalously far removed from the norm, who dressed like a paint-splashed tramp, whose temperament made close acquaintance a risky business for one's self-esteem and, perhaps the most heinous crime in the leisurely south, who worked far too hard. A rich man's hobby was only to be expected, but his was no hobby, was plain obsession.

In these six wretched years—wretched, that is, when he had not restlessly thrown Aix behind him—the offence of appearance had declined. He had begun to dress like his father, in old black frock coat and trousers and black hat. But the offence of unconventional behavior increased. These were the years when his strong fist would rattle the glasses on a café table if anyone dared to cross him, when he would leave a meal, a room, a gathering on the instant if a painter of whom he disapproved was mentioned by name, if his rare pronouncements on art were not accepted. The small boys of Aix still had work to do; if they could no longer jeer at the wealthy scarecrow, they could hang around the cafés waiting for the almost inevitable explosion.

Then came the death of old Mme Cézanne and the disbandment of the Jas de Bouffan. Hortense went back to Paris with her twenty-five-year-old son, his affection for her merely strengthened by contact with his aunt and grandmother. Cézanne joined them whenever he was in Paris and wrote affectionately when he was not. The

young Paul became his business manager: "My dear
Paul," he wrote, "I have the greatest faith in your manage-
ment of our affairs." When Cézanne discovered that Paul
took 10 per cent not only from him but from Vollard, too,
for every canvas sold, he was delighted. "My son is a great
philosopher," he announced proudly. He meant, that he
was the spit of Louis-Auguste.

For, the tension at the Jas de Bouffan removed, Cézanne
moved steadily toward geniality. When his brother-in-
law insisted that the Jas must be sold to settle the estate,
he was sad, he protested, but in the end he was the better
for it. The place had done its work for him, and that inevitable horizon of the Sainte-Victoire had kept his mind
in the right direction. Now he was driven to the Sainte-
Victoire itself to work. And to work in peace, untroubled
by the foreknowledge of a nightly return to ill feeling.
For he had taken rooms in Aix, at 23 Rue Boulégon, and
installed a housekeeper who understood him well. "I
have been to see your aunt Marie," he told his son after
one of Marie's birthdays. "This is another blight. At my
age it's most suitable to live alone and paint." And that
is what, the family put at a safe distance, he did.

5 ～～～

The second releasing event was also a death, the death
of Zola. Since sending Cézanne a copy of L'Œuvre in
1886, Zola had made no effort to approach his old friend.
He was questioned many times about the break; he was a
famous author, very much in the limelight, and the discussions which followed the publication of each of his
provocative books were headline news. His remarks about
Cézanne varied according to his mood, but he always
insisted that he meant no harm to his friend. In this he

was telling the truth as he saw it. He was not a bad man, he was simply author before friend. He had never pretended to like or even to understand Cézanne's work. He did presume to judge it, however, and claimed the right, with his reputation as art critic, to say what he thought. He went further: a success himself and famed as a penetrating psychologist, he believed that he knew a failure when he saw one. The biggest and most disappointing failure he had known was Cézanne. Cézanne had failed not only himself but all the hopes and efforts of his best friend.

There were less worthy facets of the affair. Cézanne's peasant manners and rough accent, unnoticed during the years of boyhood and youth, did not march well with the household of the great man of letters, and his crude honesty could be even more embarrassing. That Mme Zola rebelled is certain, that her husband's ancient loyalty was troubled is clear. But at the back of the business other elements stand out predominant: Zola's vanity and envy. The years of fame had distorted a youthful failing into something not far from megalomania. The widely acknowledged god of realism could not go wrong. Sadly but firmly he faced facts: Cézanne was no good; he and Cézanne had nothing in common but sentimental recollections. If *L'Œuvre* had, unintentionally, put an end to the affair, then, in the name of reality, so much the better.

This was the face that vanity put on an act dictated primarily by envy, put on so successfully that Zola had long since deceived himself into thinking it reason enough. Envy is not a feeling willingly admitted by anyone, yet Zola was envious of Cézanne as the false are always envious of the sincere. Zola knew who was the better man. He had known it ever since the meeting in school. True sincerity, like genius, escaped him. To a successful, adulated novelist the thought was inadmissible. He chose the novelist's remedy; he wrote out his dilemma; he drew a faithful picture of the man who threatened to sour all his triumphs; he then killed him. It was not true, this death. When Zola said that the later part of the life of Lantier was not based on Cézanne, he was sincere; Cézanne would never kill himself because he could never believe himself a failure. But Cézanne would interpret the book according to his own lights. Zola knew this. And Zola, bewitched by words, persuaded himself as he wrote that he was destroying his bogey.

Of course he could not. Cézanne was with him for life. He could not leave the subject alone. Years later he declared that he was "still fond of Cézanne." No doubt he was, in his way; he would have been a strange man if he had lost all feeling for Cézanne without good cause. More significant than such avowals were the moments when the journalist took charge. In an interview ten years after the publication of the book he claimed that far from traducing Cézanne in the portrait of Claude Lantier he had actually toned down the truth. "If I had chosen to reveal everything. . . !" And he explained regretfully, "Dear Cézanne doesn't think enough of public opinion, he despises the most elementary decencies, cleanliness, dress, language. Yet even this wouldn't have mattered if only my dear, great Cézanne had had genius."

He elaborated this theme publicly a few weeks later in an article in *Le Figaro*. This article, ostensibly a review of that year's Salon, was in fact a recantation. In it he finally dissociated himself from the Impressionist theories. Thirty years earlier he had written his first article in the same paper on the Salon, his article championing Manet. Now he looks round the walls. "Everything is by Manet, Monet, Pissarro!" He is horrified. "I awake and shudder.

What! Was it really for this that I fought, for this bright painting, these spots, these reflections, this decomposition of light? It is all very ugly, I find it repulsive!"

Frank words. Not less frank were his remarks on Cézanne. It was his first and only comment on the Vollard exhibition of the previous year. "We are only now," he writes, "beginning to discover touches of genius in this abortive great painter."

That same year Zola revisited Aix for the first time since *L'Œuvre* was published and for the last time in his life. He stayed with Numa Coste. As a boy, Coste had made an occasional, very occasional fourth or fifth or sixth to the trio Zola-Cézanne-Baille; he had afterward worked in the Aix academy with Cézanne. He was never an intimate friend of either Cézanne or Zola, but it was with him that Zola stayed and to him that he wrote with slightly nauseating affection on his return to Paris. The visit, Zola said, was already beginning to seem dreamlike, "but a charming dream in which I relived a little of my youth and in which I saw you again, my dear friend, you who made part of that youth."

When Cézanne heard that Zola had been to Aix, had not asked after him or tried to see him, his feelings may be imagined. They have to be imagined, for Cézanne guarded his tongue when seriously hurt. The man who had kept silent through years of bitter criticism, ridicule, and slander was not one to cry out under severer pain; he had become, at a cost, master of his feelings.

At a cost and at a gain, too; for this final cruel snub, like the remarks of Zola which his old friend read in the newspapers, produced after inevitable bitterness the resigned dignity known only to the suffering and the strong.

Six years later, September 29, 1902, Zola died tragically, asphyxiated in his bed. When Cézanne heard the

news the next morning, his face puckered like a child's
and he turned and locked himself in his studio. He stayed
there all day. When night fell he walked into the town
to the apartment of Solari, himself old, poor, infirm. They
sat together, these companions of the Zola Thursdays of
nearly forty years earlier. What they said to each other
is not known but is not difficult to guess. "Alas! How many
memories have been swallowed in the abyss of the years!"
Cézanne was to cry. But the memory of Zola remained
fresh and bright. Death wiped away every stain, for with
the common sense too often misnamed sentimentalism,
Cézanne thought only good of his lost companion. After
all, did he not owe everything to him, the man who had
thrust him into painting?

From this position, perhaps not so tenable as he
thought in his generosity, Cézanne never moved. There-
after he displayed a certain moderation in his dealings
with men. Effusive he was not, tetchy he could still be,
but signs of a sad kindliness became more and more apparent and the ironic humor overlaid for years every now
and again peeped out to explain or excuse human weak-
nesses.

This humor was soon needed. In fiction, the Zola story
would end at this point, in fact the last chapter had not
been written, and this in some ways the most unpleasant
of all. The year after her husband's death Mme Zola sold
his collection of pictures. Into the sale she put the several
gifts of Cézanne, rescued from the Médan attic and spare
bedrooms.

The Cézannes fetched a high figure, astonishing critics
and collectors by greatly excelling the price paid for the
Monets and Pissarros. They also produced a savage article
in *L'Intransigeant*. The article, entitled "The Love of
Ugliness," was written by Henri Rochefort. He attacked

Zola for foisting a daubster like Cézanne onto the public.
A portrait by Cézanne, had, he said, "cheeks sculptured
with a trowel and appeared to be suffering from eczema.
. . . Pissarro, Claude Monet, and the rest of the eccentric
plein air painters . . . are academicians, practically
members of the Institute by comparison with this weird
Cézanne."

He then used Cézanne as the stick to beat the dead
Zola, with a: "The love of physical and moral ugliness is
a passion like any other. . . . If M. Cézanne was still in
his infancy when he perpetrated these daubs, we will say
no more. But what is one to think of the leader of a school
of literature, as the squire of Médan styled himself, who
encouraged and was responsible for such pictorial insanity? And this man wrote Salon reviews in which he
claimed to direct the course of French art!"

So, six months after Zola's death, he struck again at
Cézanne from beyond the grave. He, who had been careful never to support his friend's painting publicly, was
now publicly reproached for the very act he had always
and hurtfully avoided. The irony of the situation was not
wasted on Cézanne, defensively ironical from his youth.
His strong sense of the ludicrous saved him from otherwise inevitable bitterness.

But this was not all. The article caused a stir in Aix and
unleashed a wave of malevolence which would have
sickened any man. The townspeople had never forgiven
Cézanne for being himself or the son of his father. They
disapproved of everything, of his wealth, his disdain of
ostentation, his pride, his humility, and above all of his
work. He was a disgrace to the town. The article in
L'Intransigeant gave them the Parisian authority they
needed. Hundreds of copies were bought, distributed,
read with delighted chuckles in Aix homes and at the

cafés. Sniggers and a significant wave of the paper followed Cézanne whenever he walked through the main streets. Nor was this satisfaction enough for them; they bombarded his house with copies.

Cézanne's new found calm held firm against this mass demonstration of ignorance and ill will. Never had he shown his greatness more impressively. When his son wrote anxiously from Paris to ask whether he had read the article and, if not, whether he wanted to see it, Cézanne explained with humorous brevity that the people of Aix had thoughtfully saved him the trouble: "You needn't bother to send it. Every day I find *L'Intransigeant* slipped under the door, not to speak of the copies sent to me by post!"

6

Before Cézanne reaches the last scenes of his life as painter an attempt must be made to appraise him as man. To do this, the widespread gossip about Cézanne must be examined; for this gossip, since he was unaware of most of it and refused to answer the rest, placed him once and for all with the world of his time as a boor and even a madman. And not only with the world. The gossip has been repeated, the reputation made by gossip has lived on. Much of this gossip has gone beyond recall. Most of what remains, passed on by his fellow Aixois to friends in Paris, is too cheap and degrading to be printed yet again.

But to scotch, not lies (for gossip feeds on distorted fact) but exaggerations, an example is needed. There is such an example, of an excellent kind. In Paris, in 1895, Cézanne ran into the Cuban painter, Francesco Oller, his first companion at the Académie Suisse in 1861. They had not met for years, Oller was not prospering, Cézanne's

innate kindliness broke through the protective crustiness
of his everyday demeanor. He said, why not come down
to Aix and paint? He lent him money.

The story is then taken up by Pissarro writing some
time after the event and on the sole authority of Oller.
Cézanne he had not seen. "Oller," he said, "told me of
some extraordinary things which had happened to him
with Cézanne and which suggest plainly that the latter is
a bit cracked. . . . After great tokens of affection and
that typically southern expansiveness, the all-trusting
Oller believed that he would be able to go with friend
Cézanne to Aix-en-Provence. They arranged to meet on
the P.L.M. train the next day. 'In the third-class,' said
comrade Cézanne. So the next day Oller, on the platform,
was straining his eyes, peering everywhere. No Cézanne.
Trains departed. Nobody!!! Oller ended by telling himself 'He has left believing me to have gone already,'
made up his mind and set off. In Lyons he had 500
francs stolen from his purse. Not knowing how to get out
of the mess he sent a telegram to Cézanne on the off
chance. Cézanne was at home. He had traveled first-
class!! Oller received one of those letters that have to be
read to be believed. Cézanne forbade him the house,
asked if he took him for a fool, etc. In short, an atrocious
letter. Upon my word, this is a variation of what happened to Renoir. He is furious with us all, it seems:
'Pissarro is an old fool, Monet is a sly rascal, they are no
good. . . . I'm the only one with temperament, I alone
know how to produce a red!!' "

Such was Pissarro's story, which duly went the rounds
of the painters' cafés and turned itself into history—a
more respectable and less malicious version of a thousand
others which were together to fix Cézanne the irrespon-
sible savage in the public imagination.

The facts present a different man, no saint, not easy to

get on with, yet neither villain nor madman. The "southern expansiveness" came more from the Cuban than the
man from the Midi. Oller, hard up, knew that Cézanne
was rich, had heard that he was generous in misfortune.
He exerted his charm. Cézanne responded, moved by
poverty and memories.

Twenty-four hours later, on the platform of the Gare
de Lyon, Cézanne suffered a strong revulsion. As always
since the break with Zola he regretted every impulse
leading to intimacy. He had dedicated himself to painting, he was conscious of the years running out and
dreaded any emotional entanglement which would interfere with his life's work. He hated scenes, even pleasant
ones. His fear had become a phobia. The history of the
Monet dinner was repeated in another form. But this was
far worse. At Giverny he had at least been surrounded by
painters he admired. But Oller! Horrified, he sought
sanctuary. What had he in common with Oller? What
could they possibly find to talk about for a day on end?
Haunted by thought of the long journey, of Oller's exuberant tongue, he hid himself in a first-class compart-
ment.

When he received Oller's telegram he told him to come
on to the Jas de Bouffan, where he would be put up.
Oller arrived, stayed for three weeks. By the end of these
three weeks Cézanne was close to frenzy; even at work
he was not safe from the Cuban's tongue; in the evenings
he was trapped, engulfed, bored, disgusted.

The visit ended abruptly. Oller talked too much for his
taciturn host. Worse, he tried to advise him about his
painting. Cézanne exploded. Oller lost his temper, answered back hotly and left. He was followed by this
letter: "The dictatorial tone you have been adopting
toward me recently and the decidedly offhand manner

of speech you allowed yourself to use when you left did not please me. I have made up my mind not to receive you again in my father's house. The lessons which you took the liberty of giving me have thus borne fruit. Good-by."

This is one Cézanne, accurately expressed; not the man of legend, but a difficult man who placed painting before people. But there was another Cézanne in these last years. This was the man whose models were gardeners, laborers, peasants, to whom he talked as man to man in the local patios. This was the rich man of steadily increasing fame whose best friends remained Solari and Emperaire, art's casualties; who did not, like the people of Aix, sneer pityingly at their poverty and unsuccess, but treated them exactly as if all three were the students of forty years earlier, equals in hope and aspiration.

He made many excursions with these old companions, all covering the trails laid in boyhood, most having as objective the Sainte-Victoire. On such days he threw off the years, threw off inhibitions, too. Once, for example, at the age of fifty-seven, he and Solari (a year younger) decided to climb the mountain. They set out at dawn. Cézanne was in high spirits as he climbed, pointing out all the landmarks known by heart ever since he first met Zola at school—the ravines hiding the twisting river, the great Zola dam, the Bibémus quarry they had scrambled up so often, the far hills of Marseilles sheltering the little bay of L'Estaque.

When Solari's son, who accompanied them, pointed out that the green bushes bordering the track looked blue in the early light, Cézanne chuckled ruefully. "The rascal!" he said. "He notices at a glance, when he's only twenty, what it has taken me thirty years to discover!"

The ascent made—a good three hours of stiff climbing

—they were buffeted by one of the tearing mistrals for which Aix is notorious and found shelter in the ruined Calmaldules chapel. There they contentedly munched their supplies, Cézanne and Solari *père* swapping tall stories of their boyhood feats before a son only tolerably impressed: how they had braved the sheer rock face of the Bibémus quarry, ropes disdained; how, even more daringly, they had explored again and again the horrifying Gouffre du Garagai, whose mouth gaped not far from the place in which they all sat, but had never been able to disprove the local tradition that it was the bottomless pit of the Bible.

Descending the Sainte-Victoire, they passed a certain pine. Cézanne recognized it at once; it was an old friend, a trail of strength of the trio Zola-Cézanne-Baille. Nothing would satisfy him but an attempt at this ancient yardstick. So, on the wrong side of the fifties, diabetic, after hours of steep ascent and a good hour of even more testing descent over loose rocks, he cheerfully began to shin up the tree.

He did not get very far. After an unavailing struggle to hoist himself higher he gave the tree best with a shrug and grimace. The three of them continued the descent. But before the tree was out of sight, Cézanne, with a backward look and a grin, half-sad, half-amusement at his own folly, said to Solari: "We used to be able to do that so easily!"

7 ⬿

During the early part of these last eleven years Cézanne often left Aix. In the second half of the first year, 1896, he worked at Vichy, then at Talloires on the Lac d'Annécy (where he made one magnificent landscape) and finally in Paris, where he rented a Montmartre studio. He stayed in Paris until the Spring of 1897, returned there in the autumn of 1898, worked with one of his young admirers in the Pontoise district, and did not return to Aix until the autumn of the next year.

But from this point, the autumn of 1899, he settled down in and around Aix until his death seven years later. In fact he left Aix only three times in these last seven years, paying brief visits to the Cévennes, Paris, and Fontainebleau.

This last long settlement in Aix was, of course, due partly to increasing age and ill health; he celebrated his sixtieth birthday in January, 1899, and by that time diabetes had taken a firm hold on him. But to emphasize this aspect of Cézanne would be to falsify the man. He spoke often of his failing health and strength, but his actions made nonsense of his complaints; he never spared himself and was, in the end, to kill himself by refusal to acknowledge the need for rest. If he had believed that he could improve his work by walking to the far regions of Siberia, he would have gone there without hesitation; with many grumbles, no doubt, but nothing could have stopped him.

However there was no need of Siberia, or even of Paris, Fontainebleau, or any other of the places he had worked in. "What's the use?" he wrote in humorous despair after a few weeks in Talloires. "If one has been born down south nothing else seems much good." And it was this final hardening of a conviction that had been with him on and off for most of his painting life which kept him happily in Aix—this, and the end of the domestic discord which had also played its part in driving the frustrated painter away from his home again and again.

"Wait until he finds himself," Zola had told Duret in

1870. The question, when did Cézanne find himself? has
been debated ever since. No two experts have agreed.
Cézanne the perfectionist is no help. His answer was a
blunt Never; he remained dissatisfied with his work to
the day of his death: "My age and state of health," he
told the friendly young critic Roger Marx in 1905, "will
never allow me to realize the dream of art I have been
pursuing all my life." Studying his work, even the amateur
can trace early signs of the painter whose canvases now
fetch vast sums in the auction rooms. To decide when
his "sensation" first began to take charge of these canvases is another matter.

It is perhaps impossible. Yet no one who examines the
work in conjunction with the life of the worker can avoid
the conclusion that the return to the Sainte-Victoire was
the true beginning of the victory of the painter. And the
influence of old Mme Cézanne on this return cannot be
denied. The fate of the artist rests often enough on small
and incongruous things. It would be a mistake to overrate
this influence on Cézanne—a man with his strength of
purpose would surely somehow have reached his goal.
But the fact remains that the last months of his mother's
life created such a chaos of ill-feeling in the Jas de Bouffan that the harassed and desperate Cézanne finally fled.
And he fled to the Bibémus quarry.

On the edge of this vast pit of orange-colored rock was
a small Provençal cottage, once the home of a quarry-
man. Cézanne rented it, lived there, and painted there
for months until the arrival of his mother's last days
brought him back to the Jas. In this Bibémus cottage he
found absolute peace, absolute inspiration, too. Not a
sound except the rustle of the olive trees surrounding it.
A peasant or workman the only rare visitor. Surroundings
perfectly in tune with the mood and nature of the

painter: at his back the massive wall of the Sainte-Victoire, gray, green, blue, pink, as light and shade determined, at his feet the Zola dam, where he had so often fished and swum, and the little rockbound village of Le Tholonet from which he had times innumerable begun dawn ascents of the mountain and to which he had returned tired but triumphant.

Here was peace and not only of the obvious kind. For he was in the heart of the Zola country; everything he saw, every step he took was a reliving of those years of long ago when the two or three of them roamed, talked, sang, played, untouched by premonitions of the future.

In calmness, then, Cézanne was at last ready to learn his last lesson. There it was, as it had always been, in the quarry, the houses, the scarred sides of the Sainte-Victoire before him. In his remaining years he was to paint in many places about Aix, mainly in the romantic Château Noir halfway between Aix and the Sainte-Victoire and in the studio he had built in 1901 on the Chemin des Lauves above Aix. But the lesson was learned at the quarry in the autumn of 1897; his paintings displayed it. All later work was simply a refinement, a prolonged effort to approach even closer to the truth of his "sensation" as first unambiguously expressed in the Bibémus canvases.

So at last the search of a lifetime was over; he had found himself; his "sensation" was realized in terms of color on canvas. Like all great ideas and emotions it is in essence simple. Taught by mountain and quarry, he made his pictures three-dimensional; unsatisfied with the surface painting of the day, he sought to convey depth, solidity, a feeling that what he rendered was based on, was in fact merely a continuation of an unseen primeval force.

That was the first and most easily apprehended stage. There was a further stage. Cézanne's observations and his sympathies led naturally to this stage. For years he had seen with an instinctive response of pleasure that everything which appealed specially to him in the southern scene possessed one characteristic in common; the houses at L'Estaque, Gardanne, Le Tholonet, like the face of the Sainte-Victoire and the interior of the quarry, were composed of distinctive geometrical forms. These forms both appealed to Cézanne's particular painter's eye, his vision, and would, he realized, properly applied, convey as nothing else could the three-dimensional solidity he wished to represent. And from this conception of landscape it was but a step to the building up of abstractions in place of the imitation of nature favored by the painters of the day. A Cézanne landscape is neither photographically correct nor is it an impression caught at a certain moment by a certain eye; it is a deliberate design made by the arbitrary disposition (a distortion one could say) of natural forms. His methods of indicating structure— particularly his original use of color, his system of "modulation"—have no place here. Sufficient to say that the triumph of Cézanne is that he compels his audience to realize that this artificial arrangement of abstractions represents as no other painting can do both appearance and the origin of that appearance. Hence the unique experience of a Cézanne picture, for it affords at once a sensuous pleasure and an intellectual exercise.

8 ～

Finale, 1906. The indefatigable old man is painting on. Not a day is missed. The tall white-haired figure emerging from Rue Boulégon on the dot has become an Aix timepiece. He bowls off in his hired carriage—a dilapidated affair—to studio or *motif*, not to be seen again until evening. He is still unpopular: he keeps himself to himself: but a kind of bewildered awareness of the inevitable is forcing its way into the public mind; Aix is destined to have another hero whether it likes it or not. That year comes a sign of the times; old Villevieille invites Cézanne to exhibit at the Société des Amis des Arts in Aix. Cézanne does so, describing himself in the catalogue as "Pupil of Pissarro"—his final gesture to the dead mentor. It is the first and last public appearance of his work in his birthplace.

The summer of 1906 was one of the fiercest ever recorded in Aix. The heat, Cézanne told his son, was "appalling, unbearable, stifling, oppressive." He also described it in a fashion very much his own, as "good for nothing but expanding metals, helping the sale of drinks, and bringing joy to the brewers" and, the final typical touch, "enlarging the pretensions of the intellectuals down here, a pack of ignoramuses, cretins and fools."

This was the cry of a man pushed to extremes. While his townsfolk sat at the cafés languidly drinking or lay gasping on their beds in shuttered rooms, he fought on. "I am becoming more clear-sighted in front of nature," he announced at the height of the heatwave. Time pressed. He would not give up. He made one concession only; the heat in his studio was so frightful that he drove each day to a little bridge over the Arc and painted there, where he had so often bathed and fished as a boy. The heat in the valley was prostrating but at least he could work in shadow and near water.

To try to conserve his strength he turned to water colors. He made studies cherished today as some of the finest ever known in this medium. But he did not long take this comparatively easy way out. He could not endure what seemed to him as a retreat from his life's purpose. There was no time for playing at art. He even could not find the strength for it. He caught bronchitis, he went in constant pain, his head felt terrible, congested, confused. He began to fear that he would lose his reason under the strain of working in such heat and in such pain. He was living on his nerves and, to stay at the stretch, they demanded not the soporific of water colors but the full challenge they were accustomed to. So: "Only oil painting can keep me going. I must struggle on. I simply must produce after nature."

He kept on. He beat the heat. Early in October the temperature began to fall. Then, before frayed tempers could relax, came the incident which was to shorten his life. His driver demanded more money. "I left him," said Cézanne shortly.

He began to walk to the *motif* every day. He arrived home worn out and shaking. No matter. The next day he set off again unsteadily at the same time. Nor was he content to stay by the river; the moment the great heat subsided he was off to more paintable spots, disregarding every protest of his savagely driven body: "I climb to the Beauregard area where the path is very steep, very picturesque and very much exposed to the mistral."

"I have sworn to myself to die painting," he had said. He kept his word. The heat was followed by rain. On October 15 he walked off to his *motif* as usual, pack on back. Soon after he had begun to paint, a violent storm came on. He was drenched in a few minutes but went on working, obsessed by the pressure of time passing.

The storm continued. At last he gave up for the day. He began to walk home through the hills. But for once he had taxed his strength too heavily; chilled to the bone, sodden clothes weighing him down, the pack on his back like a millstone, he struggled on, up and down the rocky paths. He managed to reach a road then collapsed. Some hours later he was found almost unconscious by the driver of a van. He was taken home and put to bed. A doctor was sent for.

The doctor told him to stay in bed, prescribed medicines. Cézanne took no notice. At dawn the next day, feeling just able to walk, he got up, brusquely dismissed his housekeeper's protestations and staggered out, pack on back once more, to his studio nearly a mile away. Somehow he forced himself up the hill to the studio. He began to work on a portrait of his gardener, determined to finish it.

That evening he arrived home in a state of collapse. He was again carried to bed. The next day, the 17th, he did not get up, but wrote to his paint merchant demanding "ten burnt lakes" which had been on order for a week.

Three days later he was still in bed. The housekeeper, worried, called in his sister Marie. Marie decided to write to her nephew in Paris: the doctor, she said, thought there was no danger, but "sometimes he is so weak that a woman can't move him . . . it took two men to get him upstairs to bed." The doctor had suggested a male nurse, but "your father won't hear of such a thing. I think your presence is necessary."

Cézanne had not been able to summon the strength to get out of bed. Actually he was rapidly growing weaker. This he refused to acknowledge. Instead, forced to contemplate a period of recuperation at home, he made his plans and conveyed them to his housekeeper.

So Marie's letter to her nephew contained, with an apologetic "You know what your father's like," an agitated warning from the housekeeper: "Your father has taken your mother's dressing room for his studio and doesn't intend to leave it for the moment."

But Cézanne was not to use this last studio. The giant spirit in that spent body urged, supplicated, commanded in vain. Two days later, October 22, before Hortense or his son could reach him, he died.

Bibliography

Manuscripts are to be found in:
    Bibliothèque Nationale, Paris.
    Louvre, Paris.
    Bibliothèque d'Art et d'Archéologie, Paris
    Musée de Vieil-Aix.
    Courtauld Institute of Art, London.

Alexis, Paul. *Émile Zola, Notes d'un Ami,* Paris, 1882.

Aurenche, Louis. "Lettre," *Tablettes d'Avignon,* December, 1932.

Barr and Scolari. "Cézanne in the letters of Marion to Morstatt," *Magazine of Art,* 1938.

Bernard, Émile. "Julien Tanguy," *Mercure de France,* 1908.

    Souvenirs sur Paul Cézanne, Paris, 1921.

Bernex, J. "Zola, Cézanne, Solari," *Les Cahiers d'Aix-en-Provence,* 1923.

Camoin, Charles. "Souvenirs sur Paul Cézanne," *L'Amour de l'Art,* 1921.

Cézanne, Paul. *Correspondance,* ed. John Rewald, Paris, 1937.

Denis, Maurice. "Cézanne," *L'Ermitage,* 1905; *L'Occident,* 1907.

Théories, Paris, 1912.

Doiteau, V. "La curieuse Figure du Dr. Gachet," *Aesculape,* 1923.

Duret, Théodore. *Les Peintres impressionistes,* Paris, 1878.

Elder, Marc. *Chez Claude Monet à Giverny,* Paris, 1924.

Gasuet, J. *Paul Cézanne,* Paris, 1921, 1926.

Gauguin, Paul. *Avant et Après,* Paris, 1919.

Geffroy, Gustave. "Paul Cézanne," *Le Journal,* 1894.

Claude Monet, Paris, 1922.

Huysmans, J. K. *Certains,* Paris, 1889.

Jeets, J. "Les Impressionistes et Chocquet," *L'Amour de l'Art,* 1935.

Lafargue, Marc. "Souvenirs sur Paul Cézanne," *L'Amour de l'Art,* 1921.

Larguier, L. *Le Dimanche avec Paul Cézanne,* Paris, 1925.

Le Blond-Zola, Denise. "Zola et Cézanne," *Mercure de France,* 1931.

Émile Zola, raconté par sa Fille, Paris, 1931.

Leroy, L. "L'Exposition des Impressionistes," *Charivari,* 1874.

Mack, Gerstle. *Paul Cézanne,* New York and London, 1935.

Maus, M. O. *Trente Années de Lutte pour l'Art,* Brussels, 1926.

Mirbeau, Octave. *Cézanne,* Paris, 1914.

Montifaud, Marc. "L'Exposition du Boulevard des Capucines," *L'Artiste,* 1874.

Pissarro, Camille. *Lettres à son Fils,* ed. John Rewald, Paris, 1950.

Provence, M. "Cézanne collégien," *Mercure de France,* 1925.

Rewald, John. *Cézanne, sa Vie, son Œuvre, son Amitié pour Zola,* Paris, 1939.

History of Impressionism, New York, 1946.

Rivière, G. *Renoir et ses Amis,* Paris, 1921.

Rivière and Schnerb. "L'Atelier de Cézanne," *La Grande Revue,* 1907.

Rochforte, Henri. "L'Amour du Laid," *L'Intransigeant,* 1903.

Venturi, Lionello. *Cézanne, son Art, son Œuvre,* Paris, 1936.

Les Archives de l'Impressionisme, Paris, 1939.

Vollard, Ambroise. *Paul Cézanne,* Paris, 1914.

Zola, Émile. *La Confession de Claude,* Paris, 1865.

"Lettre," *Le Figaro,* Dec. 4, 1867.

"Mon Salon," *L'Événement,* 1868.

L'Œuvre, Paris, 1886.

"Peinture," *Le Figaro,* Mai, 1896.

Correspondance, Lettres de Jeunesse, Paris, 1907.

Correspondance, Les Lettres et les Arts, Paris, 1908.

Index

(Italic figures denote references to the Bibliography)

"Académie," *see* Suisse, Atelier

Aix-en-Provence, 1–14 *passim*, 19, 24, 33–34, 37–38, 41–3, 46–7, 57–61, 64, 68, 73, 75, 84, 92, 99, 105, 111, 117, 122, 128, 130, 142, 153, 161, 167, 169, 171–3, 178, 180–1, 185, 187, 190, 192, 194, 201, 203, 205, 207, 209, 212, 219–20, 223–5, 228–9

Aix Academy, 24, 26, 30, 35, 40, 44, 57, *125*, *217*

Alexandre, Arsène, *200*

Alexis, Paul (1847–1901), 133, *154*

Annecy, Lac d', 224

Arc, river, 9, 24, 229

Argenteuil, 131

Arles, 13

Arosa, Paul, 136

L'Artiste, 135

Astruc, Z., 50, 54, 82, 121

Aubert, Anne, *see* Cézanne, Mme L.-A.

Aubert, Dominique, 57

Aubert, Emilie, *see* Zola, Mme F.

Auvers-sur-Oise, 108–9, 120, 136, 183, 202

Baille, Baptistin (1841–1918), 8–16, 27–8, 30, 38, 45–60 *passim*, 100, 124, *200*

Barbizon School, 111

Batignolles Group, 82, 98, 111, 114, 117–8

Baudelaire, Charles, 50, 54

Berlin, *209*

Bernard, Émile, 182, 199, *207–8*

Bibémus, quarry, 223–4, 226

Bonnard Pierre (1867–1947), *208*

Briançon, 1

Brittany, 126

Brown, John Lewis, *198*

Brussels, 188–9, *209*

Cabanel, Alexandre (1823–89), 52

Cabaner, Ernest, 133, 175

Cafés: de Bade, 61, 82; Guerbois, 82–4, 104, 107, 112, 116, 122, 159, 182, 191; Nouvelle-Athènes, 107, 122, 159

Caillebotte, G., 131–2, 196

Cassatt, Mary (1845–1926), 192–3

Cesana, 1

Cevennes, 225

Cézanne, Anne E.-H. (*née* Aubert), mother, married after birth of two first children, 3; speaks up for Paul as an artist, 26; again in '61, 44; told of liaison with Hortense, 99; deals with police over Paul's call-up, 100; keeps secret, 102; worried over grandson, 126; rents rooms at L'Estaque, 128;

Cézanne, Anne E.-H. (*continued*) and for Paul in Marseilles, 138–9; her cooking ambrosia to Renoir, 162; urges Paul to confess to his father, 164; a further appeal, 172; death of husband, 178; ignored by son, 185; dies at 82, Oct, '97, 212; her influence, 226

Cézanne, Louis-Auguste, father, born 1798, son of tailor, 1; success in felt hat business in Aix leads to banking, 2; marries Anne Aubert, 3; patient & practical, 4; plans law school for Paul, 22; buys Jas de Bouffan property, 24; at variance with Paul & Zola, 30–2; finally takes son to Paris, 32; the Banker triumphs, 43–4; favors Beaux-Arts, 47–9; portrait, 57; puzzled & disappointed by Paul's failure, 68–70; a good portrait in '66, 73; more autocratic at 69, not told of son's liaison, 99; refuses to increase his allowance, 103; his absence leads to blackmail, 122–3; farce continues, 138–9; so does quarrel with Zola, 141, 152; pride in Salon painter, 164; dies at 88, after Paul's marriage, 178

Cézanne, Hortense (*née* Fiquet), wife, Paul's model & mistress, 92–97; to Marseilles, March, '71, son born in Paris, Jan, '72, 99–104; Pontoise, 104; suffers from father-in-law's ignorance, 110; Marseilles in '78, 138; goes to ailing father Paris, 143; to Aix, 145; settled at Melun for a year, 146; loves Paris, 163; goes north with son, 169; to Gardanne from Paris, Feb, '86, 173; after prolonged stay in Switzerland, relationship with Paul disintegrates, 180; fondness for Swiss

pastrycooks, 189; dislikes Midi, Jas de Bouffan ménage divided for six years, 212; not present at husband's death, 232

Cézanne, Marie, unmarried sister, two years younger than Paul, 3; happy with him, 5; watches him at work & praises him, 24; goes to Paris with him, 32; backs him against father, 44; *Tannhäuser* portrait, 73; urges reconciliation, 164; shares house at Aix after father's death, 180; rigid Catholicism wins Paul over, 185; four hostile camps in Jas de B., 212; calls nephew to Paul's deathbed, 231–2

Cézanne, Paul, son, born Jan, 4, 1872 in Paris; illegitimacy complicates early life, 104; father's love, 143–4; used as model, 144; mother's child, 163; lives at Jas de B., 212; father's business manager, 214; called to dying father, but arrives too late, 232

Cézanne, Paul (1839–1906); born in Aix, Jan, 19, 1839, out of wedlock, 3; 1844–9: Primary School peaceful, next three years, at Ecole St-Joseph not, & trouble at Collège Bourbon; 1852–8: strong, hot tempered, but no charm, 5; hard working & suspicious, physical defence of Zola leads to devoted friendship, Baille completes inseparable trio, 7–8; unforgettable days rambling around Mont Ste-Victoire, 9–12; typical southerner, slow & stubborn, early literary leanings, 13; encouraged by Zola's enthusiasm, relapses into moodiness on his leaving for Paris, 18; 1858–61: letters to Zola discuss future as painter, hesitation in speaking to father, who insists on law studies, 21–3; joins Drawing Academy in Aix, 23, 26; refuses a banking career, father takes him to Paris, 32; 1861: finds it noisy & vulgar, likes only few Louvre pictures, 34–5; finds great change in Zola, works at Atelièr Suisse, noticed by Pissarro, 36; future as a puritanical solitary determined for life, 37; confides in Baille, 38; revival of Zola friendship, 39; works with Villevieille, up from Aix, 40; thinks of returning there, 41; destroys portrait of Zola, 42; ready to return to father's bank, 43; 1861–3: leaves after a week, works at Aix Académie from Nov to Aug, '62 & returns to Paris, where he fails Beaux-Arts exam, 46–7; father's hopes, 47–9; Manet's ascendancy, 50; meets Guillemet & Guillaumin before exhibiting at Salon des Refusés, May, '63, 51; ignored by philistine crowd, 53; influence of Delacroix, 54–6; 1863–6: alternates between Paris & Aix, ever seeking his *petite sensation*, 57; first of many refusals by Salon, portraits show signs of mature handling, 58; Zola's notoriety, intimacy with sculptor Solari from Aix, 60; Manet's *Olympia* accepted by Salon, 61; meets Manet at Café de Bade, sessions with Degas & Duranty, 62–3; portrait of Valabrègue offered to Salon, where Daubigny alone supports him, 64; Zola's articles in *Figaro*, his *Mon Salon* dedicated to Paul, 65–6; as later, bracketed with Baille, his *Confession de Claude*;

writes to Pissarro from Aix, 68; father refuses to raise allowance, 70; but increases it at Guillemet's pleading, 73; excellent portraits of father & sisters, 73; magic of Ste-Victoire begins to work, 73; 1867–9: driven to paint *plein air* as promised, 74; Jan–June, in Paris, regarded by all as strange & obstinate, 74–6; violent eroticism of Delacroix subjects, 77; starts on watercolors, 79; further Salon rejections, paints at Jas de Bouffan, often with Marion, his own secret still eludes him, 80–1; Manet's audiences at Café Guerbois, 83; Paul prefers Batignolles Group, 82; writes to Manet; Monet & Pissarro discuss color of shadow, latter's understanding & help, 86; Zola's doubts, Roux exhibits a Cézanne at Marseilles, 89; Zola publicly champions "M. Sésame," 90–2; Duret's interest, 92; 1869–71: meets Hortense Fiquet in Paris who becomes model & mistress, 92–97; Zola's marriage, 97; war sends Monet & Pissarro to England, Hortense to L'-Estaque where they stay till March, '71, 99; 1871–4: move to Marseilles before return to Paris, where son born Jan, '72, 104; Pissarro offers lodging at Pontoise, 104; "possible all sprang from Pissarro," fulfillment of *plein air* with light grays never seen at Aix, 104–5; Dr. Gachet at Auvers shows immediate interest; father, unaware of grandson's existence, refuses to increase allowance, dislike of physical touch almost a mania, 108–9; Père Tanguy exhibits Bati-

Cézanne, Paul (*continued*)
gnolles painters in Rue Clauzel, 112–13; 1874: Silvestre's Introduction to Durand-Ruel catalogue for first Impressionist Exhibition leads to acceptance. of Paul, 118–19; three canvases shown, Zola reserves criticism to "Lantier" in his *Ventre de Paris*, 121; 1874–7: return to Aix after three years, renewal of confidence despite setback, 122; Renoir's introduction to Tanguy & Chocquet leads to portrait of latter & his placing of Paul as head of impressionists, 127–9; again rejected by Salon, shows 16 canvases at 3rd Imp. Ex., 132; admiration of Caillebotte, & of Rivière, 133–4; Pissarro's friends Gauguin & Arosa collect modern artists' works, former has first Salon success, 136; difficulties with autocratic father, mother rents apartment at L'Estaque, studio in Jas de Bouffan, Hortense at Marseilles, 139; laughingstock of Villevieille's pupils in Aix, 143; Zola's financial aid for beloved son now used as model, portrait of Emperaire, 144–5; 1879–90: Apr–March at Melun, 146; rejected by Salon despite Guillemet, now Jury Member, 148; stays with Zola at Médan, paints him & slashes portrait of Mme Zola, 150; notes multiply in host's note book for *L'Œuvre*, 153; 1880–2: year at Plaisance on outskirts of Paris, 5th Imp. Ex., 154; two further Salon rejections, 156; friction with Gauguin, Duranty's posthumous novel has libelous portrait of "Maillobert," 159–60;

from Aix to L'Estaque, where Renoir joins him & paints his portrait, 161–2; accepted by Salon as pupil of Guillemet; Hortense, who loves Paris, stays with him at Médan; 1882–4: pride of father on return to Aix, paints several views of Ste-Victoire, 165; marriage of sister Rose, further rejection in Spring '83, rents house at L'Estaque, refuses Pissarro's urgent request to meet other painters, 166; visit of Monet & Renoir, 167; walks with Valabrègue roundabout Aix, finds *sensation* almost within grasp, 168; 1885–6: L'Estaque & Aix till May, strange amorous interlude, 169; June with Renoir at La Roche-Guyon, Zola his confidant at Vernon prior to Aix in Aug, 170; at Gardanne with family, 157–8; 1886: publication of *L'Œuvre* smashes 34-year trust in Zola, 176–8; registry office marriage Apr, 28, death of father six months later, 178; 1886–95: Zola's act a calamity, illusion-destroying, 179; lives with mother & Marie at Jas, further deterioration of conjugal relationship after long Swiss stay '90, 180; Pontoise lessons lead to capture of *"sensation"* by analysing *motif*, his credo to Bernard, 182; strengthened in R.C. faith by Marie, "Lantier's" studio rented '88, paints round Chantilly & Fontainbleau, Chocquet's stipulation secures *Maison du Pendu* a hanging at World Fair, his portrait painted, 186–7; Renoir rents Conil's house near Aix & keeps respect for Paul after disruption, 187;

invited to exhibit by Les XX of Brussels, 180; starts *Cardplayer* series, three years of river wandering, 190–1; Giverny autumn '94 with Monet, meets Clemenceau, Rodin, Mary Cassatt, Mirbeau & Geffroy, the critic who made deepest impression, 192–4; Caillebotte's death '93 bequeaths collection to Luxembourg, 196; Tanguy's puts six Cézanne's on low market value, 196; 1895–1906: Vollard's gallery, opened Jan, '94, lifts him to prominence, 198–9; buys Gauguin collection from Bernard, who had published pamphlet on Paul in '92, & claimed to have formulated Post-Impressionist technique, controversy over Vollard's 1st one-man Cézanne show, 199–200; '95, portrait of Geffroy, autumn in Aix till June '96, Tanguy's enthusiasm, & Nabis', Bernard's *Apothéose à Cézanne* in Salon, comparison with Verlaine, all lead to greater respect, finally agrees to exhibit, 1902, at *Salon des Indépendants,* 194–211; death of mother at 82 in Oct, '97 brings Hortense & son to Jas before final disbandment of that property, 212; son becomes business manager, 214; Vollard makes a corner in Cézannes '97, 205; Monet buys one from Chocquet's widow, 205; all his powers directed to dissection of *motif*, 206; death of Zola, after stay at Aix with Coste unbeknown to Paul, 214–17; Cézannes fetch high price at Médan sale, 218; the Oller saga, 220–3; excursions to Ste-Victoire with old friends

Solari & his son, 223; '96, June at Vichy, then Talloires, rents Montmartre studio for winter & return there a year later; with brief visits to Cevennes & Fontainebleau, remaining years in & around Aix, 224–5; finds absolute peace & quiet in Bibémus cottage, in studio on Chemin des Lauves & at Château Noir, with view of Ste-Victoire ever before him, 226–7; realizes early dream of picture not only controlled but inspired by necessities of the spirit, achieved through acceptance & final assimilation of appearance, geometrical sequence of planes in Gardanne & Le Tholonet landscapes, exhibits at *Salon D'Automne* in '04–'06, describes himself as "Pupil of Pissarro" at Aix exhibition, 229; turns to water colors to preserve strength in oppressive heat of '06, but walks to *motif* every day, "I've sworn to die painting," 230; dies Oct 22, 1906, 232

Domiciles in Paris:
 1861: Rue Coquillière, later Rue des Feuillantes, 32
 1865–7: Rue Beautrellis (No. 22)
 1870: Rue Notre-Dame-des-Champs (53), 97
 1871: Rue de Chevreuse (5, with Solari)
 1872: Rue de Jussieu (son born), 103
 1874: Rue de Vaugirard (120), 126
 1875: 1888–90: Quai d'Anjou (15, "Lantier's"), 128, 187
 1877: Rue de l'Ouest (67)
 1880–2: Rue de l'Ouest (32), 154

Cézanne, Paul (*continued*)
  1892: Rue des Lions-St-Paul (2)
  1895: Jan–June, Rue Bonaparte
  1896–7: Rue des Dames (Montmartre Studio)
           Rue St-Lazare (73), 225
  Domiciles in Aix:
  1859–89: Jas de Bouffan, *passim*
  1899–1906: Rue Boulegon (23), 214, 228
  Paintings:
    Bathers, 189: Cardplayers, 190; Château Noir, 227; L'Estaque & Marseilles, 100–1, 161–2, 164; Gardanne, 173; Gardener, 231; Jas de Bouffan murals, 57; Still Life, 58, 199–200
  Pictures:
    Une Chaumière à Auvers, 189
    L'Enlèvement (The Rape) (1867), (Coll. Zola), 76
    Étude de Paysage, 189
    Halle aux Vins (Coll. Pissarro), 103
    L'Hermitage à Pontoise, (1875) "Intoxication" & "The Wine Toddy," 90–1
    The Judgment of Paris (1860), 76
    The Orgy (1872–3), 76
    La Maison du Pendu (1873), 120–1, 186, 189, 205
    La Maison du Père Lacroix, 106
    Street in Pontoise, 106
    The Temptation of St Anthony, 76
    A Modern Olympia, 120–1
    Vieille Route à Auvers, 106
    View of Auvers (1874), 106
  Portraits (Family):
    Father, 56, 73
    Marie (Tannhäuser), 56, 73
    Rose (with doll), 56, 73

    Hortense, 97–8, 165, 180, 190
    Paul, 144, 190
    Uncle Dominque, 56
    Achille, Emperaire (1866–8), 144–5
    Victor Chocquet (1877 & 1889), 132, 187
    Gustave Geffroy (1895), 194
    Antoine Valabrègue (1866), 64
    Émile Zola (1861 & 1880), 41–2, 151
    Mme Zola (1880), 150
  "*le motif,*" 151, 167, 182, 206, 209, 229–30
  "*ma petite sensation,*" 46, 57, 158, 168, 181, 183, 189, 201–2, 226–7
Chantilly, 136, 186, 190
Château Noir, 227
Chocquet, Victor, 127–8, 134, 145, 161, 172, 185–7, 192, 202
Chocquet, Mme, 127, 145, 186, 205
Clemenceau, Georges, 192, 195
Commune, the, 102, 111
Conil, Maxime, 165, 187
Corot, J.-B. (1796–1875), 108, 117
Coste, Numa, 217
Courbet, Gustave (1819–77), 50, 61, 87, 127, 202

Daubigny, Charles (1817–78), 64, 113
Daudet, Alphonse, 192
David, Louis (1748–1825), 48
Degas, Edgar (1834–1917), 61, 63, 83–5, 111, 117–19, 191–2, 201–3
Delacroix, Eugene (1798–1863), 50, 54, 56, 58, 74, 127, 202
Denis, Maurice, 207–8, 211
Dierx, Léon, 133
Durand-Ruel, Paul, 116, 129, 132, 162
Duranty, Edmond (1833–80), 50, 54, 63, 82–4, 93, 121, 159

Duret, Théodore (1838–1927), 92, 113–14, 117, 129, 175, 225

École des Beaux-Arts, 46–49, 54, 65
École Polytechnique, 30, 46
Emperaire, Achille (1829–98), 144–5, 223
Evénement, L', 60
Exposition Universelle, Paris, 75, 79–80, 87, 186, 205

Fantin-Latour, Henri (1836–1904), 54, 117
Figaro, Le, 65, 90, 200, 216
"Fiquet, A.," 141
Fiquet, Hortense, see Cézanne, Mme Paul
Fiquet, M. (father), 94, 143
Fontainebleau, 111, 136, 186, 190, 205, 225
Franco-Prussian War, 98–9, 102

Gachet, Dr. P.F., 108–112, 120, 154, 161
Gachet, Mme, 113
Gardanne, 173, 190, 228
Gauguin, Paul (1848–1903), 36, 136–7, 156–9, 182, 188, 199, 200, 207–8
Geffroy, Gustave (1855–1926), 193–5, 200
Gilbert, Joseph (1808–84), 143
Giverny, 191–2, 194, 222
Groux, Henri de, 189
Guillaumin, Armand (1841–1927), 51, 53–4, 60, 76, 86, 88, 96, 107, 109–10, 112, 117–18, 126, 128, 132, 136, 143, 186, 188, 196, 202
Guillemet, Antoine (1841–1918), 51, 59–62, 71–3, 76, 81, 102, 117, 125, 148, 150–1, 162, 165

Heymann, critic, 202
Huysman, J.K., 156

Impressionism, 108, 111, 120, 127–30, 132, 135–6, 166, 176, 188, 191–2, 195, 200, 205, 216
Impressionist Exhibitions, 1st: Apr, 1874, Soc. Anon. des Artistes, Peintres etc. three canvases shown, 119–21, 126, 186; 2nd: Apr, '76 declined by P.C.; 3rd: Apr, '77, 16 works shown, 129–32, 159; 4th: '79, P.C. decides not to show, 161
Intransigeant, L', 218–19
Issy, 136

Jas de Bouffan, 24–5, 57, 71–3, 80, 99–100, 126, 139, 141, 142, 164–5, 173, 180, 184, 190, 212, 214, 222, 226
Julian, École, 208
"Justine," 20

"Lantier, Claude," 176–7, 200–1, 216
La Roche-Guyon, 170, 172–3, 187
Lauves, Chemin des, studio, 227
L'Estaque, 99–101, 104, 128, 130, 139, 141–43, 161, 166–7, 182, 190, 228
Le Tholonet, 227–8
Les XX de Bruxelles, 188–9
Louis Napoleon, 52, 98, 115
Louvre Museum, 33, 35, 54, 67, 132, 200
Luxembourg Museum, 35, 196

Mack, Gerstle, xii
Manet, Edouard (1832–83), 50–6, 60–7, 83–86, 106, 111, 116–18, 120, 129, 136, 159, 196, 216
   Pictures by: Le Balcon, 51; Le Bon Bock, 117; Déjeuner sur l'Herbe (Le Bain), 53; Olympia, 61, 64; Spanish Guitar Player, 54
Margerie, Roland de, xii
Marion, Fortuné (1846–1900), 81
Marne, river, 190
Marseilles, 4, 30, 89, 99, 102
Marx, Roger (1859–1913), 226

Maus, M.O., 188
Maus, Mme, 189
Médan, Zola's house, 149, 157, 163, 171, 174, 178, 192, 218–9
Mellerio, André, 196
Melun, 146, 149
Mirbeau, Octave, 193
Monet, Claude (1840–1926), 85–6, 111, 116, 119, 127–9, 132, 134, 136, 149, 154, 167, 175, 188, 191, 193–6, 200, 202, 205, 216, 218–19, 222
    Pictures by: *Bd des Capucines*, 120–1; Rouen Cathedral series, 191
Montmartre, studio in, 225
Morisot, Berthe (1841–95), 51, 117–18, 127, 132
Mortier, A., 91
Mürger, Henri, 21
Musset, Alfred de, 10, 20

Nadar, photographer, 107, 119
"Nana," Zola's boat, 171
Natanson, Thadée, 200
Nieuwerkerke, M. de, Director Beaux-Arts, 64, 91

Oise, river, 106, 113, 190
Oller, Francisco, 36, 220–2

Paris, *see also under* Cézanne, 23–68 *passim*, 75–98 *passim*, 108, 111, 135, 156, 180, 186, 188, 190–1, 195–204, 208, 225
Pissarro, Camille (1830–1903), 36, 51, 59–60, 68, 70–1, 73, 76, 85–8, 104–08, 111–14, 116–20, 125–6, 128–30, 132, 136–7, 148–9, 154, 156–9, 161, 183, 186, 188, 191–2, 195, 198–9, 201–3, 205, 216, 218–19, 221
Pissarro, Mme, wife, 104, 117
plein air painting, 23, 85, 101, 105, 219
Pont-Aven, 208

Pontoise, 104–9, 114, 130, 136, 156, 183, 202, 225
Post-Impressionists, 156, 197, 199

Renoir, P.A. (1841–1919), 86, 99, 103, 111, 116, 118–19, 127, 132, 134, 136, 148, 154, 161–2, 167, 170–1, 173, 175, 187, 191, 194–6, 201–2
Rewald, John, xii
Rivière, G., 133–4
Rochefort, Henri, 218
Rodin, Auguste (1840–1917), 193
Roussel, K.X., 208
Roux, Marius (1838–1905), 80

Sainte-Victoire, Mont, 8, 19, 24, 45, 48, 58, 74, 79–80, 165, 167, 214, 224, 226–8
Salons: des Indépendants, 211; des Refusés, 52–3, 55, 59, 61, 64–5, 67, 90–91, 119, 156; Officiel, 48–52, 59, 61, 64, 67–70, 80, 87, 90, 97, 103, 116–17, 119–21, 125, 128–30, 136–7, 148–9, 154–56, 159, 165; 1st acceptance, 162–64
Seine, river, 149, 190–1
"Sésame, M.," 90
Seurat, Georges (1859–91), 199, 207
Signac, Paul (1863–1935), 207
Silvestre, Armand, 116, 121
Sisley, Alfred (1839–99), 117, 119, 127, 188, 194, 196
Societé anon. des Artistes etc., 119
Solari, Émile, 223–4
Solari, Philippe (1840–1906), 60, 76, 87, 103, 175, 218, 223–4
Suisse, Atelier, 35, 40, 44–5, 50–1, 220
Switzerland, 180, 189–90

Talloires, 224–5
Tanguy, Julien "Père," 111–13, 127, 149, 195–6, 207–8
Temps, Le, 200

Toulouse-Lautrec, Henri de (1864–1901), 189
Tribune, La, 92

Valabrègue, Antoine, 55, 57, 59, 61, 64, 78, 89, 100, 113, 125, 167, 173
Vallier, P.C.'s gardener, 231
Van Gogh, Vincent (1853–90), 13, 36, 56, 108, 111, 150, 188–9, 207
Verlaine, Paul, 209–10
Vernon, 171
Versailles, 35, 111
Vichy, 224
Villard, Nina de, 133
Villennes, 171
Villevieille, J.F. (1829–1915), 40, 140, 143, 229
Vincent, Joseph, 120
Vollard, Ambroise, 197–201, 204–07, 211, 214, 217
Voltaire, Le, 154
Vuillard, Edouard (1868–1940), 208

Zola, Émile (1840–1902), schoolboy friend of P.C. & Baille at Aix, 6; writes Paul letters from Paris, 19–22, 27–29; a true Parisian, 33–4; rarely sees Paul, 38–9; sits for portrait, 41–2; back to Aix with Baille, 45; discussions on Manet, 55; *La Confession de Claude,* 1865, dedicated to Paul & Baille, 59, & *Mon Salon,* a pamphlet, to Paul, 66; writes on art for *Figaro,* 65–6; hears from Valabrègue, 78; sociable, unconvinced about Paul's career, 70–71, 76, 88–9; writes for *Tribune* & answers Mortier's "M. Sésame" article on Salon des Refusés, championing Impressionists, 90–92; refuses to give Duret Paul's address, 92; attempts to soften Paul, 92 ("Wait until he finds himself," 92); marriage, 97; *Le Ventre de Paris* (1873), introduces "Claude Lantier," silence on Impressionist Exhibition, 121; L'Estaque summer '77, meets Paul's appeal to help Hortense, 139–41; asked to loan Still Life to 4th Imp. Ex., 147; settles at Médan, where Paul paints portraits, 149; Mme Zola tries to clean him up, 151–2; keeps notes on artist's curious behavior, 153; Paul writes meekly "to one who still consents to be my friend," 153; Impressionists enlist his help, but misses chance to hail Post-Impressionism, 155–6; primes Guillemet to accept Paul for Salon, successfully, 162; letters from Paul, 165; more feverish letters on strange clandestine liaison, 170–1; Paul uneasy at Médan, 172; reads *L'Œuvre* & is shattered, 176–9; vanity & envy lead to misrepresentation; true sincerity like genius escape him; last stay at Aix with Coste a cruel snub to Paul; death from asphyxiation, Sept 29, 1902, 214–17
Zola, Émile, *née* Aubert, mother, 6
Zola, François, father, builder of dam at Aix, 6
Zola, G.E. Alexandrine, *née* Meley, wife, 97, 151–2, 175, 215, 218
Zola, Barrage, 6, 80, 223, 227